WORKBOATS

AN ILLUSTRATED GUIDE TO WORK VESSELS FROM BRISTOL BAY TO SAN DIEGO

WORKBOATS

AN ILLUSTRATED GUIDE TO WORK VESSELS FROM BRISTOL BAY TO SAN DIEGO

Archie Satterfield

Illustrations by Walt Crowley

SASQUATCH BOOKS

Seattle

Printed in the United States of America

Cover and interior design: Kris Morgan

Library of Congress Cataloging in Publication Data

Satterfield, Archie
    West Coast workboats: an illustrated guide to work
vessels from Bristol Bay to San Diego / Archie Satterfield;
illustrations by Walt Crowley.
        p.   cm.
    ISBN 0-912365-51-X: $11.95
    1. Work boats—Pacific Coast (U.S.)   I. Title
VM351.S27 1992
387.2'26'09795—dc20   92–19507
                                                      CIP

Sasquatch Books
1931 Second Avenue
Seattle, Washington 98101
(206) 441-5555

CONTENTS

CONTENTS

SAFETY WORKBOATS

LARGE WORKBOATS

INTRODUCTION

When I moved to the West Coast many years ago, I recognized only one kind of workboat; I was familiar with tugs because they moved my ship around when I was in the Navy. I knew nothing about the others. Trawlers, trollers, gillnetters, and crabbers were as foreign to me as objects used in Mayan religious ceremonies. Over the years I've learned the identity and purpose of working boats along the coast the way most newcomers do: by osmosis. Many books about pleasure boats and ships are available, but workboats have been largely ignored. That is why I wrote this book.

I have always liked workboats because they do real things. They push and pull ships around. They are used to catch fish and to save lives. They carry cars, food, and people. They are used to clean up messes and they haul people out to build things or to fix them. They provide the muscle along the coast and do the dirty work that must be done.

Like many laborers, they are usually taken for granted by the public.

Perhaps it has something to do with my work ethic, but I love to watch workboats and have been guilty of sitting in waterfront restaurants and giving more attention to boats than to my dining companion. Pleasure boats aren't nearly as interesting to me, and I haven't bothered learning to sail because I could never be content sailing around awhile and then having to come back; if I can't go on a voyage to the Seychelles or some other exotic port, I don't want to go at all. Compared with the rugged, no-nonsense workboats in this book, pleasure boats seem frivolous. I would feel conspicuous owning one.

Workboats are a direct reflection of the place where they are used. A sailboat or a powerboat looks the same whether it is in Florida or Vancouver, but a workboat tells you what kind of industries you'll find in a region: fishing, logging, or shipping.

In recent years the dividing lines between species of boats have blurred. Several kinds of boats, such as the smaller Coast Guard and police boats, use identical hulls, and only the insignia painted on later sets them apart. Fishermen can buy a seiner/long-liner/crabber, all in the same boat. Builders have perfected hull types that work equally well in calm inland waters and in the rough seas of the Gulf of Alaska. In the case of fishing boats, at least you can still look at the rigging and know what kind of work the boat does. That isn't true of many other boats, because they are so easily adapted to a wide range of chores. An unfortunate result is that many of the newer boats aren't as interesting to look at. They've become the nurses' shoes of the world afloat: efficient, effective, and economical, but not very distinctive.

Another blurring of identification is the distinction between boats and ships, and I freely admit that I have pushed the limits of the "boat" definition in some cases. Several definitions of boats and ships are given, but my favorite, delivered to me in Navy boot camp, is that a ship can carry a boat, but a boat can't carry a ship. Purists will point out that I have included some ships here, such as the buoy tender, the dredges, and the factory processor. My response is that they perform duties that can as easily be assigned to boats and that their size is not at issue.

One temptation I had to overcome was the almost overwhelming urge to include many historical workboats. For example, I have been in love with the *Star of India* in San Diego's harbor since first seeing it many years ago. This love became almost obsessive when I found out that it was part of the Alaska Packers Association Star Fleet and that, laden with Alaska salmon, it had sailed in and out of Semiahmoo Bay on the U.S.–Canadian border. Only the numb at heart would not find such a craft beautiful. However, it doesn't appear here because it is no longer in commercial service.

Several other beautiful old vessels can be found all along the coast, and boats, particularly those made of wood, are like some wines and some peo-

ple: They become infinitely more interesting as they age. After much deliberation, I decided to include only vessels that are in active service, such as the gracious old *Virginia V*, the last remnant of Puget Sound's Mosquito Fleet. For the same reason, I omitted the historic Monterey boats, originally used in the sardine fishery but now relegated to pleasure boating and sports fishing; they are no longer true workboats.

Nearly everywhere I went for information, I was met with courtesy and enthusiasm. People who work with boats

have a relationship with them that I think is quite unlike that of pleasure-boat owners, something like the difference between a person who owns a dog as a pet and a person who owns a dog to herd sheep or pull a sled: Both love their animals, but in quite different ways. The pet owner pampers the dog and loves to show it off. The owner of the working dog tends to take the animal for granted, like an old sweater or an old friend, and seldom mentions it in conversation.

—Archie Satterfield

3

The tug heaves against its load. The booms begin to move, groaning, behind the chugging weight of the tug; Hank and Lee hurry to secure the couplings between the great carpets of logs. "Keep on the bounce," is Hank's advice, "or they'll go rollin' under you. It maybe don't look it, but it's safest to keep on the bounce." Ken Kesey, Sometimes a Great Notion

LOG BRONCS AND POND BOATS

Workboats don't come much smaller than the industrious little vessels you see in log ponds outside sawmills and at docks where ships are loaded with logs bound for the Orient. They are called boomboats, log broncs, or even "booming beavers." The original boomboats were no more than two logs lashed together and an outboard motor. Some still aren't much more than that. Most, however, do have a place to sit that offers some shelter from the weather for the operator while he or she goes about the job of sorting logs according to length and quality, makes up log rafts, and pushes logs into position to be hoisted aboard a ship or taken into a mill.

Some log broncs have "dogs," or teeth, on their bow so the boat can "bite" into the logs for a good grip. Others have rounded bows and rely on the operator's dexterity to push the logs where they are supposed to go.

The uninitiated might think these boats are fun and easy to run, but their operators are true specialists. They usually have had several years of experience working as deckhands on tugs and as boom men in log ponds, complete with pike poles and the loggers' traditional hobnail, or "cork," boots.

Most boomboats have no rudder or

reverse gear because the propeller is mounted on a Z-drive that permits the thrust to be directed through 360 degrees. Newer boomboats have diesel engines and power-assisted steering. The wheel has a knob on it to indicate the direction in which the propeller is pointed.

The next step up the pond-boat evolutionary ladder is the small tug requiring a skipper and deckhand. While there is no one typical log tug, most are over 20 feet long. An example is the *Harken 2*, which operates on the Fraser and Pitt rivers at Port Coquitlan, B.C. The steel boat is 28 feet long, with an 8-foot beam and a 4-foot draft. It has distinctive teeth on the bow so it can get a good grip on logs to prevent them from slid-

ing or slipping beneath the boat. Like the log bronc, the tug is used to sort logs and make up log rafts.

These boats are becoming increasingly rare in the United States due to a substantial decrease in the number of old-growth trees harvested and restrictions on the sale of raw logs to foreign countries. Most pond sorting has been replaced by land-based sorting yards where logs are trucked rather than floated and towed to their destination. U.S. pond boats are being sold to Canadian operators whose logging areas are not accessible by road and who do not face similar economic and environmental restrictions.

Pond Boat (Log Tug) *Harken 2*

Length ....28 feet

Beam ....8 feet

Draft ....4 feet

Propulsion......................................Diesel; 165 HP

Speed ....8 knots

Construction ....Steel

Crew..2

The next largest tugs working logs in sheltered water are in the 35- to 50-foot range. These tugs are powerful enough to tow booms out into salt water, yet small enough to work easily in ponds making up rafts and tows. The *Port Susan*, for example, is owned by Dunlap Towing Company of Everett, Washington. It is large enough to be comfortable for two crew members and offers some shelter from the weather and a place to brew a pot of coffee. It is used mostly in the harbor and in the lower reaches of the Snohomish River in Washington State.

Log Tug *Port Susan*

Length...42 feet

Beam...16 feet

Draft ....6 feet

Propulsion......................................Diesel; 350 HP

Speed ....9 knots

Construction ....Steel

Crew..2

LOG RAFTS

When you hear boatmen talking about boom sticks, swifters, and pike poles, you'll know you're listening to men who work with log rafts. Log rafts, or booms, are a common means of moving logs in British Columbia, Puget Sound, and on the Columbia River. All along the Pacific Coast, in rivers and in harbors, you'll see log rafts tied to pilings or buoys or being towed by small tugs.

Log rafts are held together by boom sticks and swifters. Boom sticks are logs about 65 feet long with holes drilled in each end, through which boom chains are passed to hold the logs together. The average length of a log raft in Puget Sound is six boom sticks, or nearly 400 feet. That's between 250,000 and 300,000 square feet of wood! River rafts are sometimes twice as long but not quite as wide. A log tow is made up of several rafts and is pulled by a large tug.

Boom sticks can last many years without being replaced, but sometimes new holes must be drilled when time and rough treatment take their toll. Before the holes are drilled, the logs are floated to determine which side is going to face upward; then they are drilled with a large powered auger. Boom sticks that don't float with the holes straight up and down are a real problem.

Some rafts are one log deep and flat, but increasingly they are being made of bundles of logs that are assembled in a rack on the shore, lashed together with swifters — which are steel cables — and then pushed into the log pond for the tugs and boomboats to assemble into rafts.

Each region has its own style of making up rafts. In Canada, for example, boom sticks are part of the log inventory and are not reused. On the Columbia River, the prow of the raft is made of two boom sticks in the shape of a V. The aft end of the raft is blunt. Strangely, the aft boom stick is called a header.

Rafts are left in salt water for limited lengths of time because of the ever-present teredos—the shipworms that live in salt water and eat anything made of wood that hasn't been treated with creosote or some other noxious preservative. After six weeks or so in salt water, the booms must be towed into fresh water, which kills the teredos.

Sometimes log rafts are stored for years before use, in which case they start growing a crop of moss, grass, and bushes. If left long enough, they will sprout young trees.

The log rafts you see on inland waters may be on their way to sawmills or pulp mills, and many are on their way to the Far East via freighters. (Recent state and federal laws restrict the export of raw logs from the U.S.) Some logs have their bark peeled off before they're processed or loaded onto the ships. The bark is ground up into dust for gardens.

Like most tugboat work, towing log booms isn't a job for people in a hurry. Few tugs tow at more than 1 or 2 knots because of the strain on the raft. Pulling a log boom too hard could literally pull it apart. Also, the overall size of a raft creates high resistance in the water, which in turn limits towing speed. In all coastal waters, the effect of tidal currents must be considered when towing. In the Columbia River, tugs tow upstream on the flood, or incoming, tide and downstream on the ebb, or outgoing, tide. Small tugs have no choice but to pull over and tie up when the current is running hard against them. A tow can take several days or even weeks to reach its destination. Skill, patience, and a love for not getting anywhere too soon are the marks of the tug skipper who is a good log tower.

Pleasure boaters have been known to ignore or fail to recognize the towing lights or the black diamond on a tug's rigging that signals it has a log boom under tow, and have either run across the tow cable or run onto the log boom itself, neither of which improves the cable or the offending boat. A story, perhaps an urban folktale, persists that a Puget Sound powerboater, coming home after dark, beached himself on a log boom, couldn't get the tug crew's attention, and had a long, slow ride from Seattle to Tacoma.

This "cigar" raft was made up for towing in the open ocean. Frequently used in the past, such rafts have been replaced of late by self-unloading log barges.

SMALL WORKBOATS

PILOT BOATS

Certain ships entering and leaving North American ports must be under the direction of a licensed pilot. These pilots must pass a series of Coast Guard examinations that test their knowledge of local waters as well as their ability to maneuver ships of all sizes.

Pilots are used on all ships of foreign registry, on U.S. and Canadian ships that have gone to a foreign port and are returning, and on a variety of other vessels. Pilots have even been hired by sailboat owners to bring their vessels into unfamiliar waters. The state sets the tariffs that pilots may charge.

When called upon to navigate a ship in or out of a harbor, a pilot is taken out in a boat, called a pilot boat for obvious reasons, to meet the ship at a specified location. The pilot goes aboard while the ship is under way, climbing a ladder, which in heavy seas almost invariably ensures a drenching. Once aboard, the pilot serves as an advisor to the master or captain with respect to the navigation and maneuverability of the ship until it is safely moored or anchored in port.

During a typical year, Puget Sound pilots assist between 8,500 and 8,600 ships. They work 14 days on and 14 days off, traveling between Port Angeles and Puget Sound ports. Pilots are used on outbound as well as incoming ships.

Pilots usually board ships outside a line of demarcation, which is where the Coast Guard's rules for navigation on international waters and those for inland waters meet. Each harbor in the United States and Canada has one of these imaginary lines, usually between two buoys or other navigational devices.

In San Francisco, pilots meet ships 11 miles offshore to bring them across the bar into San Francisco Bay. San Francisco is the only port on the West Coast where the pilot boat might lie offshore for 24 to 36 hours rather than be dispatched from shore for each assignment. The San Francisco association owns two 85-foot boats, the *San Francisco* and the *California*, and a 65-footer, which fills in when needed. On Puget Sound, ships come down the Strait of Juan de Fuca under the skipper's command to Port Angeles, where the pilot comes aboard. Ships bound for Victoria and Vancouver, B.C., pick up their pilots just inside Race Rocks on the north side of the Strait of Juan de Fuca. In Long Beach, California, pilots go about a mile and a half beyond the sea buoy (the first navigational aid outside the harbor) to pick up the 9,000 or more ships they assist each year.

Pilot boats and their crews must be tough. On the Columbia River, for example, one group of pilots takes ships across the treacherous Columbia River Bar, which has earned the title Graveyard of the Pacific. On the way out to the ship, the pilot boat must withstand a constant pounding. Once the ship has cleared the bar, the bar pilot disembarks and a river pilot comes aboard and takes the ship to ports from Astoria to Portland.

No demarcation lines exist in Alaska, where all waters are subject to the Coast Guard's international rules.

Few pilots have harsher working conditions than the Middle Rock, Inc., pilots association of Homer, Alaska. This group provides pilots for all of the domestic tankers coming in and out of Prince William Sound and the Alaska pipeline terminal at Valdez. Initially tanker captains brought their ships into the Valdez dock unassisted, but after a tanker rammed the dock and caused considerable damage, the Coast Guard required that pilots be put aboard at the entrance to Valdez Arm. Then, on March 24, 1989, Good Friday, the *Exxon Valdez* struck Bligh Reef, creating a monstrous oil spill. New regulations followed requiring pilots to go aboard farther out; oil tankers are now piloted to and from

Cape Hinchinbrook, which is 67 miles from Valdez.

Ferrying pilots such a distance to meet tankers created the need for a boat that could take a terrible beating from Alaskan weather and seas. It had to be durable; the flow of oil from the pipeline literally depends on the boat because if the boat can't transport the pilots, no ships can enter or leave the port.

The pilots association's contract went to Munson Manufacturing of Edmonds, Washington, which had established a reputation for building durable aluminum boats. The small company had built several Coast Guard patrol boats and police boats for cities all over America and had perfected a type of hull called the Hammerhead, which rode well, didn't broach easily, and kept the spray to a minimum at high speeds.

The resulting 62-foot boat, the *M/V Columbia*, is one of the toughest and most sophisticated workboats ever built.

It routinely goes out into the Gulf of Alaska in 60-knot winds and 25-foot seas in temperatures as low as 10 degrees below zero. It has to function normally when coated with several inches of ice. Like a jet aircraft, it has double and triple redundancies for safety. An example is the reinforced hull and double bottoms with rip-away skegs; if the pilot boat hits an iceberg head-on and the outer hull rips, the inner hull should remain intact. The *M/V Columbia* has triple radar systems, and its windows are electrically heated to keep ice from forming. During the winter months, the deckhands are outside with plastic hammers, chipping the ice away from the deck. Fortunately, sea ice peels away more easily than freshwater ice.

Since the *M/V Columbia* can't be shut down for normal maintenance and repairs, it has its own repair shop and comfortable accommodations for up to 18 passengers. It has four bunks in two large staterooms with full-size showers.

Virtually nothing is heard about ships' pilots until they make an error, and these errors can be spectacular. In 1978, a ship under the guidance of a pilot named Rolf Neslund rammed West Seattle's Spokane Street Bridge and left it stuck permanently in the up position; an entire section of freeway and a new bridge were built as a result.

A vessel with a pilot aboard will always fly the international code flag "H," a red-and-white flag (see page 109).

Pilot Boat *M/V Columbia*

Length	62 feet
Beam	20 feet
Draft	3 feet
Propulsion	Diesel; 2 × 900 HP
Speed	20 knots
Construction	Aluminum
Crew	2

Mon Dieu, votre mer est si grand et mon bateau est si petit.
Breton prayer

SMALL WORKBOATS

CREW BOATS

Crew boats are a common means of transportation along the coasts of British Columbia and Alaska, where roads are few. They take millworkers to and from their jobs, ferry relief crews to tugs working offshore, carry log buyers and scalers out to log booms to inspect them, and perform a wide variety of other chores. Crew boats, sometimes called taxi boats, are utilitarian in design and appearance, boasting little more than a cover overhead, a bench or two with cushions, and a powerful outboard.

Most newer ones are built of aluminum, and after a few years they bear the scars of being banged against docks, pilings, other boats, and log booms. The accompanying illustration and specifications describe a 24-footer owned by Harken Towing of Port Coquitlan, B.C., which can carry up to 10 passengers.

Crew Boat *Laura Lee*

Length	24 feet
Beam	8 feet
Draft	2 to 3 feet
Propulsion	Gas 454 Chevrolet Marine; 300 HP
Speed	28 to 30 knots
Construction	Aluminum
Crew	1

Harbor police boats are often based on a design similar to that of crew boats.

©WC'92

> *There is nothing—absolutely nothing—half so much worth doing as simply messing about in boats . . . or with boats . . . . In or out of 'em, it doesn't matter.*
> Kenneth Grahame, *The Wind in the Willows*

KICKER BOATS

What a dull place our inland waters would be without the ubiquitous kicker boat. Each region has its own rites of initiation that turn newcomers into residents, and in the maritime Northwest, two of those rites are fishing for steelhead in the winter and fishing for salmon in a kicker boat.

How did kicker boats get their name? The original skiffs were powered by a rudimentary one-cylinder motor that delivered power to the propeller in spurts, or kicks, as it putt-putted along. Kicker boats are perhaps the most nondescript and unobtrusive of all the boats in this book because they are nothing more than a small boat powered by an outboard motor. They range from 14 to 16 feet long and have a pointed bow and a square stern for the motor. They seat two to three people, or more if the occupants are small or on good terms. The originals were wood, of course, and had a good deal of character. Now they are typically made of aluminum. They are built with reasonably high sides so they will ride high in the water and won't take random waves over the side or transom.

Kicker boats are everywhere around sheltered waters; on rivers, in harbors and bays, on lakes and the sheltered waters of the Inside Passage. They are honest members of the workboat class, used for handtrolling for salmon and for transporting fishermen between larger boats and the shore. You will see them riding on the decks of many fishboats heading to Alaska for the summer. Boathouses rent them by the hour or the day, but you usually must provide your own modest outboard motor, anywhere from 15 to 30 horsepower; 20 is certainly sufficient.

Anyone who has spent a few hours in a kicker has his or her own favorite stories. The author, for example, held up ferry traffic for perhaps 20 minutes at Mukilteo, Washington, because the motor he borrowed died directly in front of the ferry dock.

A friend told of sitting in a fog bank jigging for salmon when his companion looked up with an expression of stark terror on his face: Their kicker had drifted right up to the bow of a freighter that, fortunately, was anchored. "I looked around and all I could see were big numbers on the bow — six, seven, eight — and I almost fainted," he said.

The sea is no playground to the small-boat independent fisherman; it is his dark camerado and wily adversary;
the meat on his table and the gasoline in his car come from the sea; if it fails him he is grounded upon hard times.
Ralph Friedman, A Touch of Oregon

FISHING BOATS

TUNA CLIPPERS

Some of the most beautiful commercial fishing boats in the world are the sleek, sharp-bowed tuna seiners. They are seen occasionally sailing out of San Diego and other Southern California ports. Their lines are so long and graceful that they can be mistaken for yachts. Anyone who has fished in Alaskan waters, lived in the cramped quarters on the boats and processors, and dealt with the cold, wet weather will think these vessels are yachts because they are so spacious; many have individual cabins and air-conditioned living spaces. Although their proper name is tuna seiner, many people still call them clippers.

A tuna seiner's greyhound look is not for aesthetic purposes alone, because speed is of utmost importance for tuna fishermen. Schools of the fish commonly called albacore tuna, yellowfin, skipjack, bigeye, and Northern bluefin are *fast* swimmers, and once a school is spotted, obviously the *fastest* vessel gets to the tuna first. It is big business; clippers are expected to return home with a catch worth $1 million or more in the hold. American-made boats have the reputation of being the fastest in the world and have set records for payload; the largest single catch on record was made in September 1991 by the American-built

Silla Pioneer, owned by Silla Trading of Seoul, which caught 510 short tons in one set and successfully refrigerated the entire catch.

When the clipper nears known fishing grounds, a member of the crew goes aloft to the crow's nest to search for signs of tuna, and other crew members line the rail looking for a cluster of birds or disturbances on the surface made by the feeding fish. When they are searching at night, the lookout occasionally flashes a spotlight across the surface, looking for the phosphorescent glow that signals a disturbance in the water. Sometimes small airplanes are used to spot fish and to lead the boat to them, but this obviously can be used only when the boat works close to shore. Clippers in the South Seas are increasingly carrying helicopters that go aloft to help spot fish.

Once boats have found the fish, the next problem is getting the purse seine into the water while still running at 16 or 17 knots. This requires not only strong nets but booms, winches, and other equipment sturdy enough to withstand the stress.

First, a skiff is lowered into the water and kept snug against the clipper's stern while the seine and its cables are attached

to it. Then the skiff and net are released, and the seine is stretched out between the clipper and the skiff. A fence is formed by the buoyed and weighted sides of the net. The mast man on the clipper gives directions to the wheel man in the skiff to keep the net around the school of fish.

The crew tries to herd the fish into the net by dropping firecracker-type explosives called cherry bombs into the water, by racing the skiff or speedboat back and forth, and by hammering on the sides of the vessels. A clipper may use one skiff and up to three speedboats.

The school of fish is corralled as quickly as possible, with the skiff holding its end of the seine in position while the clipper makes a wide turn. When they meet, the skiff passes a purse line from its end of the seine to the clipper's power block. Reeling the line in through the block closes the bottom of the net under the fish, forming a purse, or basket. As the net is pulled in through the block, the purse gets smaller until the fish can be collected. If the catch is especially large, the seine will be divided into sections before being taken aboard. It is important to haul the fish out of the water as quickly as possible so as not to attract sharks.

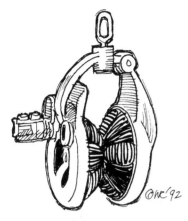

Puretic power block

The most popular tuna clippers are built by Campbell Shipyard in San Diego. These boats fish off the coasts of Africa, South America, New Zealand, and Australia; in the Indian Ocean; and all around the Pacific Rim. In the 1980s, Campbell introduced the Super Pacific Class, more commonly known as the Superseiners. Their greater speed and fuel efficiency and faster net setting solidified their dominance in the field. This new class of vessel followed several years of design changes and tank testing, and the result is a boat that saves up to $1,000 a day in fuel, has much faster freezing capability, and has an antiroll tank for improved stability over previous designs.

In spite of the dominance of American tuna-boat builders, the tuna-canning industry is almost a thing of the past in North America. Most tuna fishing and canning now are done on the west side of the Pacific Rim and along the coast of the Indian Ocean. As a consequence, few tuna clippers are seen along the West Coast anymore.

Tuna Clipper/Superseiner

Length	220 to 256 feet
Beam	40 to 44 feet
Draft	18 feet
Propulsion	Diesel; 2,600 HP; bow thruster 500 HP
Speed	17 knots
Construction	Steel
Crew	15 to 19

Reeling in a tuna seine

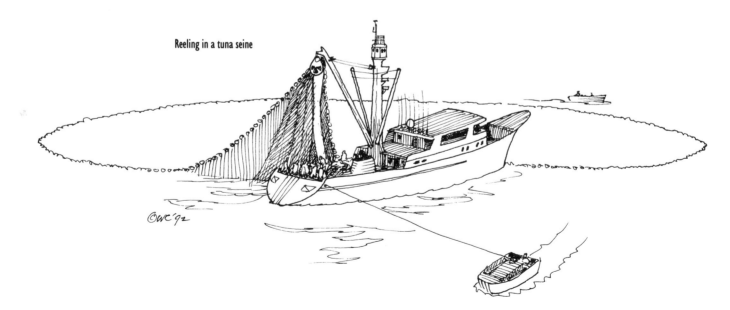

All dories start with a flat bottom and grow out of it, as it were. Regardless of whether the dory is put together right-side up or up-side down, the bottom comes first. Put sides on the bottom, and the boat is built. It is almost as simple as that.
John Gardner, The Dory Book

OREGON DORIES

One of the most beautiful stretches along the Oregon coast is the Three Capes Scenic Drive, a loop road off Highway 101 from Tillamook south to Pacific City. The three capes are Cape Meares, at the mouth of the Tillamook River, Cape Lookout, and Cape Kiwanda. The latter's multicolored sandstone outcropping looms above a perfectly flat beach, and just offshore a few hundred feet is a haystack rock with a small arch carved into it. Cape Kiwanda juts out far enough to shelter a small bay from the winds and swells from the north and northwest.

When pioneers in the area discovered that schools of salmon came in close to the Oregon shore to feed, they went down the nearby Nestucca River in rowboats and then rowed north to Cape Kiwanda. It was a long, hard row against the seas and the north wind; soon fishermen began launching directly off the beach south of Cape Kiwanda. Their boats were mostly 16- to 18-foot double-ended dories with rocker bottoms, curved like a rocking chair so they could spin around easily. Some had outboard motors, but the fishermen didn't trust them in the surf and relied on their oars to get them out into the open ocean.

In the early days, before the Three Capes road was built, boats were hauled to the cape with horse-drawn wagons. Later, when fishermen had motor vehicles but still no roads or bridges, they improvised temporary bridges across the Nestucca River by tying two boats in the river and running planks across them so they could drive over in trucks loaded with boats. Eventually roads came, but the fishermen stuck with their traditional method of getting in and out of the surf.

This continued until 1961, when two fishermen from Portland showed up with a 15-foot, square-sterned boat with a 25-horsepower motor. Nobody thought the outsiders knew what they were doing, and the locals stood around waiting to see how they would handle themselves after the expected dunking. But it didn't happen. The fishermen pushed their boat out into the surf and leaped aboard, and when the breakers lifted them free of the bottom, they gave the motor full power and roared through the breakers and out to sea. When they returned, they stopped outside the breakers and waited until the right wave came along, gave the motor full throttle again, and literally surfed in atop the wave. At the last second the fishermen shut off the motor, flipped it up, and shot up on the beach, high and dry. The local fishermen were astonished and immediately realized that their method of launching and landing their dories had changed forever.

This incident revolutionized the Cape Kiwanda dory design and use. Today the Pacific City dory is made of plywood, is 20 to 22 feet long, and has a flat bottom. It is powered by an outboard motor anywhere from 70 to 150 horsepower, although most are in the 70- to 88-horsepower range. A 70-horsepower motor will hit top speeds of around 30 miles an hour, and an 88-horsepower will hit 40 miles an hour.

Now you can watch the launchings and landings from the beach, and almost all do it the same way. The fishermen back their trailers into the water, push the dories backward into the shallow water, and then park their pickups and trailers in the lot above the beach. They turn the dories around, push them out into the surf, and stand at the stern waiting for the right wave. When it comes, they launch the dories into the wave and let the wave roll beneath them. This drops the stern, and the fishermen climb aboard just in time for the stern to rise and lift them. Then they start the motor and go out through the breakers and into the ocean.

The return is more dramatic and is almost identical to the landing described above. The dories hit the beach at about 20 miles an hour and slide several boat-lengths onto the sand, making them easy to load onto the trailers. It is believed that this kind of commercial fishing is done in only one other part of the world, off a beach in Australia.

Victor Learned used to be a dairy farmer in the Pacific City area, but now he is known as the best builder of Pacific City dories and almost always has one or two under construction in his barn. In 1991 he charged $4,000 to build one that was 21 feet 3 inches long, with a bottom of 5 feet 6 inches at its widest. The boats are built of ⅜-inch marine plywood, with a ⅜-inch sheet on the sides and two sheets of ⅜-inch plywood bonded together for the bottom. Learned covers the bottom with a ⅛- to

³/₁₆-inch coat of fiberglass to protect it from landings on the sand for up to 10 years. The dories come equipped with a console panel for instruments and floor-boards; otherwise, the boats are bare.

Onto this basic model, owners add their motors — a few use inboard-outboards — and their fishing gear. Most are rigged up as one-person trollers with stainless-steel main lines strung to a hy-draulic reel and outrigger poles on either side. Strung to the main line are 8 to 12 lines and lures at various depths, anchored by a cannonball lead weight at the end.

Most fishermen go after salmon and bottom fish. Some still go out for tuna, but since tuna run 20 to 30 miles off-shore, the fishermen have to be certain of the weather before going out that far in a 22-foot open boat, usually with no radio.

Between 300 and 400 dories are in use off the Cape Kiwanda beach now, but fewer than a quarter of those are ac-tually used for commercial fishing. Very few of the owners are able to support themselves on fishing alone because of severely shortened seasons.

Each July the Oregon Dory Celebra-tion is held in Pacific City with a parade, a bazaar, a dance, and a dory race.

Oregon Dory

Length	22 feet
Beam	5 feet
Draft	4 to 6 inches
Propulsion	Outboard or inboard-outboard; 70 to 150 HP
Speed	To 30 knots
Construction	Marine plywood, fiberglass-coated bottom
Crew	1 or 2

PURSE SEINERS

By far the most common type of net seen along the West Coast is the purse seine, which is designed to catch fish that are found near the surface: some species of salmon, mackerel, tuna, and herring. Purse seine operation is described in the essay on tuna clippers (see pages 17–18) and is essentially the same no matter the size of boat and net. Purse seine nets are one of the most adaptable types of fishing gear and can be found on small skiffs as well as on tuna clippers. More salmon are caught by purse-seining than by any other method of fishing.

Two basic kinds of equipment are used to retrieve the seine, and both came into use during the 1950s to replace hauling in the net by hand. Some older boats still use a power-assisted drum on the stern to pull in the seine, but most use the power block.

The original power block was invented in 1954 by a Yugoslav immigrant named Mario Puretic, who was fishing in Southern California and getting tired of fighting the huge nets. His first model was a rope-driven block and pulley secured to a boom over the boat's work area. The seine lead was started through the block, and the crew operated the block by its continuous rope, a far easier

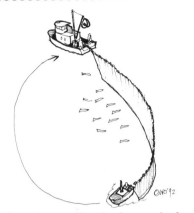

chore than pulling in the nets by hand.

Even though the power block's potential seemed obvious to many, old-timers tended to be conservative, and Puretic could find no support in California for his invention. However, a group of fishermen from Puget Sound and British Columbia heard of the power block and drove down to San Pedro to watch Puretic demonstrate it. They were impressed and told a two-year-old Seattle company named MARCO (Marine Construction and Design Company) about it. The company made a deal with Puretic. Fishermen were so anxious to get the power block, now armed with hydraulic power, that MARCO had to set up a by-the-number system of filling orders, something like standing in line at the butcher shop. More than 20,000 power blocks are in use today.

It is worth noting that the power block is given credit for virtually saving the tuna fishing industry. Before the block's invention, tuna were caught only with hook and line. With the power block, tuna clippers could use enormous nets that weighed tons when loaded with fish.

As is the case with so many new fishing boats, a purse seiner can be identified by its ever-present power block rather than by the shape of its hull. Another way to identify a seiner is to look for the skiff that is stowed on the aft deck when the seine is aboard and is out on the water when the seine is being set. The skiff is used to pull the seine out and bring the end back around to the boat to form the purse. When the net is reeled aboard, the skiff pulls against the stern of the fishing boat so it doesn't get tangled in the net.

Purse Seiner, Hansen-built

Length	52 feet
Beam	17 feet
Draft	5 feet
Propulsion	Diesel; 550 HP
Speed	9 knots
Construction	Fiberglass hull, aluminum house
Crew	4 to 5

FISHING BOATS

TROLLERS

Not all commercial fishing boats are what they may seem at first glance because many serve dual purposes, allowing their owners to fish for more than one species. You may see a boat rigged with tall poles for salmon trolling that also has the chute of a long-liner on its transom. And sometimes a boat is used for both gill-netting and purse-seining. The rigging tells the story; the size and shape of the boat itself are usually secondary.

Trollers are the most versatile fishing boat because they can go after several kinds of fish — all species of salmon, tuna, and bottom fish — without having to change gear. Some clear their decks of fishing gear during the winter and fish for crab. You will see trollers all through the sheltered waters of British Columbia and southeast Alaska and along the Oregon and California coasts, often several miles offshore, wherever the schools of salmon and tuna are found. Most have some kind of refrigeration aboard, from several bags of ice to sophisticated refrigeration systems, to keep fish fresh until their return to port or until they sell their catch to a tender.

Whenever you see those tall poles standing beside the mast, you know without doubt that the small boat is used for trolling. The wooden, fiberglass, or aluminum poles (also called booms or outriggers) stand straight up and are lashed to the mast when not in use. While fishing, they are suspended over the side of the boat at roughly a 45-degree angle, with stainless-steel fishing lines trailing behind. Many boats use four poles — two long ones and two short ones — with the longer poles positioned at a slightly lower angle so the lines will be less likely to become entangled. Others use only two poles, with one set of lines at the very tip and another running about midway out.

The poles are secured to the boat with brackets on the rails when in use, and when not in use they rest in the crosstree below the masthead. There is no set rule for their length, although generally the poles are roughly the length of the boat itself.

Each pole has a powerful stainless-steel line of up to 1,000-pound strength that is reeled in and out by its own gurdy (winch), which is powered by hydraulic pumps, an electric motor, or a power takeoff. Each steel line has from 5 to 10 leaders with lures attached at intervals. All the lures are kept at the desired depth by weights, usually cannonball-shaped lead or iron sinkers hooked ahead and to the rear of the armada of lures. Floats are usually attached to one of the two lines on each side as buoys, so the outboard lines will stay far enough from the inboard lines to prevent tangling.

The boats look for fish in traditional feeding grounds and by using sonar equipment that signals the presence of schools of fish. A bell attached to each pole rings when a fish is hooked. With no way of knowing how many are hooked, the fisherman hauls the line in with the gurdy, and as the leaders and lures come aboard, they are unclipped and hung or coiled on the stern to be baited and snapped on when the line goes back out again. When the leader with the fish comes alongside, the fisherman stops the gurdy and hauls in the leader by hand, and then brings the fish aboard with a gaff. This is the most tense time for the fisherman, because if a fish is going to get away, it usually will be during this process.

Lures are brightly colored spoons, plugs, or hoochies shaped to wriggle and dart as they move through the water. Sometimes a flasher — a long, flat piece of shiny metal shaped so it will flip back and forth like a fish — is placed ahead of the lure. Most lures have a single hook.

The gurdies make it possible for fishermen to work alone. When two people work a troller together, they are often a married couple or a fisherman accompanied by a family member or friend.

Traditional trollers are wooden double-enders. They are still seen all along the West Coast.

A recent change in boat design and construction has turned new boats into hybrids that do double and triple duty as purse seiners, long-liners or trollers, and crabbers. Owners can easily and quickly offload one set of gear and install another to get much more use from the boat than if it were designed for only one type of fishing.

Typical of this trend is the seiner/long-liner/crabber built by Hansen Boat Company in Marysville, Washington. It has a large area on the stern for purse seines, crab pots, longlines, and automatic hook-setting machinery, as well as two large holds for the fish. The boat is available in 50-foot to 125-foot lengths.

Troller

Perhaps more than any other workboat, trollers defy specifics. They vary widely in almost every statistic, so these specifications are by necessity general.

Length ....25 to 45 feet

Beam...8 to 18 feet

Draft ....2 to 9 feet

Propulsion ....Mostly diesel, some gas; 40 to 300 HP

Speed ....8 to 20 knots

Construction ....Mostly wood, some steel and aluminum

Crew...1 or 2

FISHING BOATS

TRAWLERS

Trawlers are a close relative of purse seiners. While purse seiners fish near the surface, trawlers fish closer to the bottom in search of flatfish, cod, haddock, shrimp, and rockfish. Boats used as trawlers must have a large open deck area for net handling and storing. Consequently, many trawlers double as crabbers and long-liners.

The standard trawl net is cone-shaped and is towed behind the boat at the speed and depth determined by the species of fish being sought. The depth the net reaches is controlled by weights and floats. The mouth of the net is kept open by devices called doors attached just ahead of the net. The doors are shaped so that as they are pulled along, resistance from the water pushes them outward, keeping the net mouth open. The net may be 100 feet wide across the opening and 150 feet long.

The most distinctive piece of equipment visible on the deck of a trawler is the large net drum, almost always on the stern, which brings in the heavy net

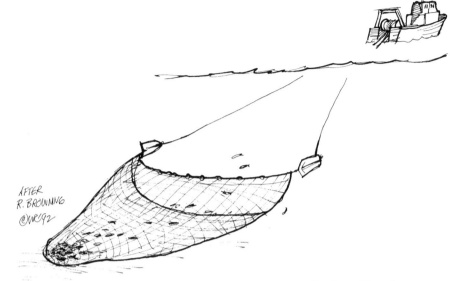

AFTER R. BROWNING @NRC92

and stores it when not in use. Some trawlers, especially the newer ones, have a gantry or crane on the stern with pulleys to raise the loaded end of the net over the transom as it is brought aboard.

Specifications for trawlers are approximately the same as for large crabbers and long-liners. A crew of three or four can operate a small trawler. If the catch is to be processed and frozen on board, the crew size increases.

Factory Trawler

Length	135 feet
Beam	30 feet
Draft (maximum)	17 feet
Propulsion	Diesel; 1,175 HP
Speed	11 to 12 knots
Construction	Steel
Crew	24

> *In steering a small boat before a heavy gale don't look back—it may disconcert you. Fix your eye*
> *on a cloud or breaking sea right ahead and keep her straight—if you can.*
> F. A. Worsley, *Shackleton's Boat Journey*

FISHING BOATS

CRABBERS

Of all the kinds of fishing, crabbing in Alaskan waters is the most dangerous. Alaskan king crabs are caught in the Gulf of Alaska, the Bering Sea, and along the Aleutian Islands. Winds of more than 100 knots are common, and frequent storms create some of the most hazardous boating conditions in the world. Every year lives are lost as boats founder or crew members are washed overboard. But men and women keep going out on the crabbers for one simple reason: They can make a lot of money quickly. While the glory days of the 1950s and 1960s, when crab boats produced almost instant millionaires, are gone, big money can still be made. The income is less today, however, and the crabs are neither as large nor as plentiful as they once were because the resource has been heavily harvested for several years.

Crabbers must be sturdy to withstand the heavy seas. The pilothouse and fo'c'sle are kept well forward, leaving plenty of space aft. The clear deck area is used for storing the pots during transport and for wrestling them aboard to be emptied before rebaiting and winching them overboard again. Danger comes when ice forms on the stacked pots, creating a towering weight on the stern of the boat.

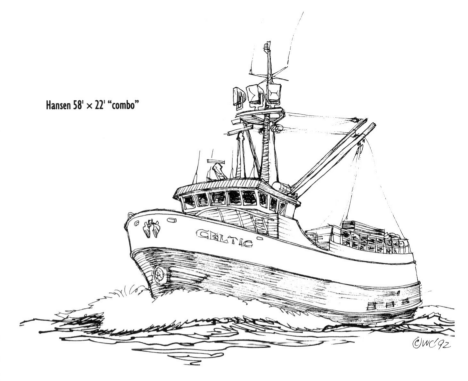

Hansen 58' × 22' "combo"

Crabbers that venture out into the Bering Sea are typically more than 100 feet long. Smaller crabbers stay closer to shore.

Hansen Boat Company of Marysville, Washington, builds boats that do triple duty as seiners, long-liners, and crabbers. They come in five lengths: 50, 58, 70, 105, and 125 feet. The 58-foot model can carry 140,000 pounds of salmon or 70,000 pounds of crab.

Crabber, Hansen Boat Company

Length	58 feet
Beam	22 feet
Draft	10 feet
Speed	11 knots
Propulsion	Diesel; 500 HP
Construction	Steel hull, aluminum house
Crew	5 to 6 seining; 3 to 4 crabbing; 7 to 8 long-lining

CRAB POTS

Crab gear hasn't changed much since the crabbing industry began in the 1950s. Like other kinds of fishing, crabbing has become more mechanized, but the basic implement, the crab pot, is essentially the same after four decades. Crab pots are built in two general sizes: 6 ½ feet or 7 feet square. Both are 34 inches high. They weigh 650 pounds empty, and when they are loaded with crab and winched aboard, they can weigh between 1,500 and 2,000 pounds.

Crab pots have a steel frame and nylon webbing. They are baited with frozen chopped herring stuffed into bait jars drilled with holes or packed into a porous bait bag suspended inside the pot. Codfish and other scrap fish are also used as bait. The crabs are lured by the smell. In 1992, new pots cost $300 to $350 each.

A crab pot's location is marked by a large float attached to it with a line. The dangerous and laborious work of dropping pots to the bottom and retrieving them has been automated. The pots are put overboard by cranes and lowered to the bottom, which can be 1,000 feet deep or more. When the pots are retrieved, one machine hoists them aboard while another coils the lines.

These same pots—with slightly larger openings—are used by some factory trawlers to catch black cod, also called sablefish.

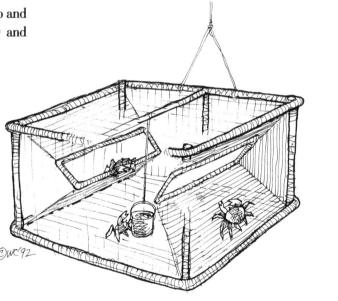

There was no part of the hook that a great fish could feel which was not sweet-smelling and good-tasting.
Ernest Hemingway, The Old Man and the Sea

LONG-LINERS

©WC '92

Boats used as crabbers are often used as long-liners as well. Long-lining, a method of catching bottom fish introduced on the West Coast primarily for halibut, is now also used for cod and black cod. It is a saltwater version of what is known in other parts of North America as a trotline, a line from which several baited hooks dangle while it is left in position for several hours.

The commercial fishing version uses a single line to which detachable leaders are attached at various intervals, the most common being 40 inches. The longlines are reeled out over the stern of the boat. A float or flagged buoy is set at each end of the line. The two major kinds of long-lining are subsurface and bottom. A subsurface longline has floats or buoys spaced along it to keep the line at a specific depth; a bottom longline has anchors to hold the line close to the bottom and buoys to keep the hooks off the bottom. These buoys also serve as markers for retrieval.

It is conceivable that a single longline could have 30,000 hooks, which would make it 19 or 20 miles long, but the maximum length is usually between 5 and 6 miles. More often, shorter lengths

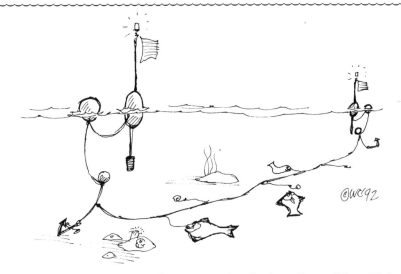

are used. The crew will lay out four or five lines that form a box or intersect each other.

The chore of baiting all those hooks and retrieving them led to the invention of automatic hook baiters and haulers that bring in and coil the ground line. Other machinery includes automatic bait cutters and baiters that load hooks randomly with squid, mackerel, and herring.

A typical factory long-liner is the 135-foot *Frontier Spirit*, built by MARCO (Marine Construction and Design Company), which can freeze and hold 300 metric tons of fish before returning to port. The processing crew removes the heads and guts and freezes the catch.

Smaller long-liners (35 to 50 feet) are distinguished by a shed on the stern where the crew stands when baiting hooks, and a line chute through which the longline is released.

Factory Long-liner
Frontier Spirit

Length	135 feet
Beam	30 feet
Draft (maximum)	17 feet
Propulsion	Diesel; 1,175 HP
Speed	11 to 12 knots
Construction	Steel
Crew (including processors)	24

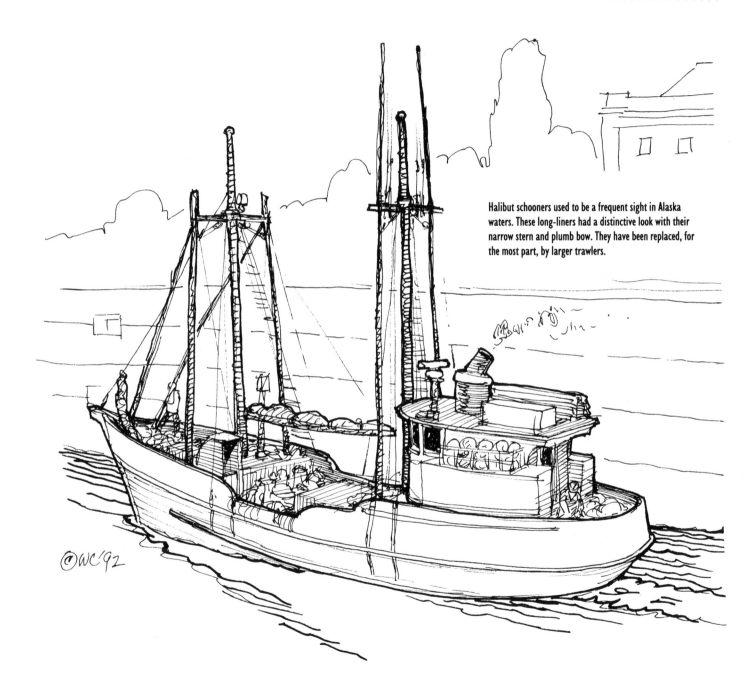

Halibut schooners used to be a frequent sight in Alaska waters. These long-liners had a distinctive look with their narrow stern and plumb bow. They have been replaced, for the most part, by larger trawlers.

©WC'92

34

Salmon and the Columbia River are synonymous. Originally there were more chinook, coho
(here called silvers or silversides) and steelhead trout than in any other river system in North America.
Anthony Netboy, *Salmon: The World's Most Harassed Fish*

FISHING BOATS

GILL-NETTERS: BOWPICKER

LONG ISLAND II

©WK '92

Gill-netters are another hybrid of the commercial fishing industry; their purpose isn't always clear by looking at their shape. Almost every type of small fishing boat seen along the West Coast has been or can be used for fishing with gill nets, including pleasure boats, rowboats, and all manner of scows.

In spite of this, a type of gill-netter exists on the Columbia River that is distinct from all other boats. It comes in a variety of lengths but is distinguished by its "bowpicker," which hauls the net aboard at the bow. Many bowpicker gill-netters, most of which were built in small boatyards along the banks of the Columbia River and on Puget Island, can still be seen on the river, in Willapa Bay, and in Grays Harbor. A smaller version, hardly more than a 12- to-16-foot skiff with an outboard motor, is used on shorter trips in sheltered waterways along Puget Sound and the Inside Passage.

Gill-netting was introduced to the Columbia River in 1853, a bit ahead of salmon canning. The first gill-netters were called Whitehall skiffs; they were brought from Maine with nets that had been developed in New England to catch Atlantic salmon. When the United States's first salmon cannery was built at Eagle Cliff, near Skamokawa, Washington, in 1866, the prototype of the Columbia River gill-netter was brought up from California. It was an open sailing boat about 22 feet long, rigged with the mast far forward.

This prototype gradually developed into the bowpicker configuration to keep the nets as far away from the sailing gear as possible, a design that worked equally well along the Canadian coast and in Bristol Bay, Alaska. When engines replaced sails, boat designs had to prevent the net from becoming fouled in the propeller. The originals were usually of double-end dory design with no shelter. When the sailing gear was abandoned, most boat owners added a small wheelhouse toward the stern but left the forward area open for net retrieval and storage.

The bowpicker design has staying power. Many newer gill-netters have been built with the design intact, but the boats are larger, more stable, faster, and much more comfortable. Net reels powered by hydraulics or power takeoffs from the engine have replaced hauling in the net by hand.

Necessity dictates form and function in fishing gear, and using gill nets, which entangle a fish by its gills, is the most logical way to fish in the murky waters of rivers and in shallow saltwater inlets where the fish migrate and where the current is strong. Those fishing the Columbia River must contend with both the river flow and the rise and fall of the tides. When the tide comes in, the river below Bonneville Dam is stopped, and sometimes its flow is reversed. Gill-netters work only when the tide is on the ebb and the river is flowing out to sea. This means that night fishing is common.

The river above Tongue Point in Astoria, Oregon, is partitioned into drifts, or sections reserved for fishing groups called snag associations (the river below Tongue Point has never been worked by the associations and has always been open to all who fish). The lower Columbia River is the only place in the world where drifts are recognized, as they have been since the 1870s, although they have no basis in law. They were formed as a means of keeping the riverbed clear of debris that would clog or damage the gill nets, which were originally knitted by hand and were more valuable than the boat itself.

The snag associations equalized fishing opportunities for members by rotating assignments and by drawing lots. There was no way to guarantee that each member would catch the same number of fish, but the associations did give each the same opportunity.

In gill-netting, a float or buoy with a battery-powered light is attached to one end of the gill net. Fishermen take their boats to the drift zone, drop the buoy, and then head slowly across the channel, paying out the net. Floats hold one edge on the water's surface, and lead weights keep the other edge down, forming a porous wall through which salmon will try to swim. When the fish hit the net, their heads can get through only as far as their gills, which become entangled in the net, and they drown.

Once the net is strung out in a more or less straight line, the fisherman cuts the boat's engine and floats downstream to the end of his drifting zone, or set, which may take an hour or longer. Then the net is hauled in over a drum that operates off the boat's engine and into a work area that is illuminated by a floodlight. As the net comes aboard, salmon, as well as debris, which damages the net, will be removed in a tedious process. Gill-netters rarely have refrigeration.

The maximum net length permitted on the Columbia River is 250 fathoms (1,500 feet), and the net openings, or mesh size, are determined by the season and restrictions imposed by the departments of fisheries of Oregon and Washington under the terms of the Columbia River Compact. Fishing boats must share the river with seagoing ships, and since ships have the right-of-way, the nets must be reeled in when a ship approaches. In the early days, when all nets were taken in by hand, fishermen sometimes had no choice but to cut the net and make a run for their lives when a ship came bearing down on them.

Gill-netter

These specifications are very general and apply mostly to the older gill-netters found in the sheltered waterways of Puget Sound, the Inside Passage, and the Columbia River.

Length .... 20 to 32 feet

Beam .... 7 to 16 feet

Draft... 1 to 4 feet

Propulsion .... Gasoline or diesel; 50 to 200 HP

Speed .... 7 knots

Construction .... Wood, some aluminum and steel

Crew... 1 or 2

Salmon caught with gill nets usually bear the marks of the net on the back of the head and just above the gills. The size of the mesh is regulated so that smaller fish can escape.

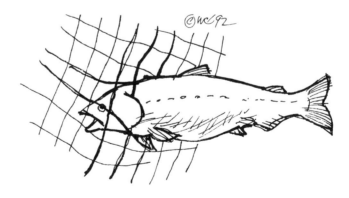

Fish are where one finds them.
Anon.

GILL-NETTERS: BRISTOL BAY

One of the world's most famous and productive fishing grounds is Bristol Bay, off the west coast of Alaska between the Alaska Peninsula and Cape Newenham. Since the late nineteenth century, a variety of fishing boats have been developed to catch the millions of sockeye that run each summer. One of the offspring of those early and dangerous days is the Bristol Bay gill-netter, a wooden double-ender designed to go out only short distances from the shore cannery or tender. The original boats were powered by sail. Engines were not allowed on Bristol Bay fishing boats until 1951.

In the early days, the Bristol Bay gill-netters were allowed to stretch their nets across the mouths of rivers, but after that was outlawed in the face of declining salmon runs, they used the same method as river gill-netters. Today they set their nets by dropping one end attached to a buoy and then unrolling the net across the current. After several hours, they reel in the net. The typical boat has a roller across the transom and a powered net reel driven by a belt or chain, or hydraulic power. The fish are picked out of the net by hand. Most of the catch is frozen rather than canned.

Today, a special fishing license is required to fish in Bristol Bay. A license for gill-netting can cost up to $200,000. The days the boats are allowed to fish are now restricted in order to control the salmon runs. The length of the boat and the net, as well as the mesh openings, are also closely regulated. Currently, a Bristol Bay gill-netter cannot exceed 32 feet in length. The mesh size is $5\frac{3}{8}$", and the net can be no more than $28\frac{1}{2}$ mesh deep. The net cannot exceed 150 fathoms (or 900 feet) in length.

Many of the old gill-netters are still in use all along the North Pacific coast, from Northern California to Bristol Bay.

Bristol Bay Gill-netter

Length	22 to 32 feet
Beam	7 to 12 feet
Draft	1 to 3 feet
Propulsion	Gasoline or diesel; 50 to 140 HP
Speed	7 to 22 knots
Construction	Wood; aluminum, fiberglass
Crew	1 or 2

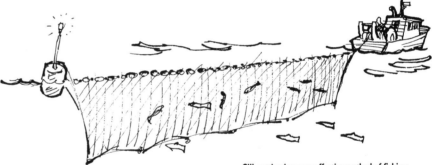

Gill-netting is a very effective method of fishing, particularly in or near large rivers, where water tends to be murky and the net less visible to the fish during daylight. The Fraser and Skeena rivers in British Columbia and the Copper River and Bristol Bay in Alaska are all highly productive gill-net fishing areas.

REEF NETS

Fishing with reef nets is one of the few Native American methods of catching salmon that is still being done the way it was for centuries before Europeans came to the Northwest. Most of the reef fishing in Washington is done along the western side of Lummi Island and in the San Juan Islands, particularly off Stuart and Lopez islands.

The original reef nets were made of willow-bark twine and were more or less flat except for one end, which was shaped into a bag to trap the fish. One net—usually about 30 feet long—would be suspended between two canoes and anchored with stones. Six or seven men in each canoe held the net in position with lines. A lookout, usually the most experienced fisherman, stood in each boat and signalled when to pull up the net after the salmon swam inside. The fish were then dumped into one of the canoes, and the net was lowered again.

A variation of this method was used in deeper waters. To the canoes and net described above, the Native American fishermen added side and bottom lines that stretched several feet away from the canoes and nets. The nets were strung on lines that were anchored to the bottom with large stones and then sloped up to the level of the net's opening. Floats on the surface and lines anchored to the bottom with stones held them in place, forming a U-shaped chute. The fishermen would keep the side lines free of kelp and seaweed so the fish would be certain to see them. The bottom lines would sometimes have bunches of grass tied to them to create the illusion of the bottom. The fish would see the bottom and side lines and, in avoiding them, would swim directly into the waiting net.

Today's reef fishing gear is only slightly more modern. The boats are usually about 40 feet long and 8 feet wide and are little more than rafts with room for nets and a place to store the fish. The nets are secured with four concrete anchors that weigh from 1 to 5 tons. The boats have a wooden tower that is about 15 feet high. The nylon nets are black so the salmon can't see them easily.

The lookouts stand in the towers, and when they see salmon enter the net, they shout to haul up the net. Most of the boats have gasoline or electric engines to hoist the heavy nets as rapidly as possible.

The season is from midsummer until fall, depending on the size of the run. The number of commercial licenses for reef fishing is limited to 50 in Washington State.

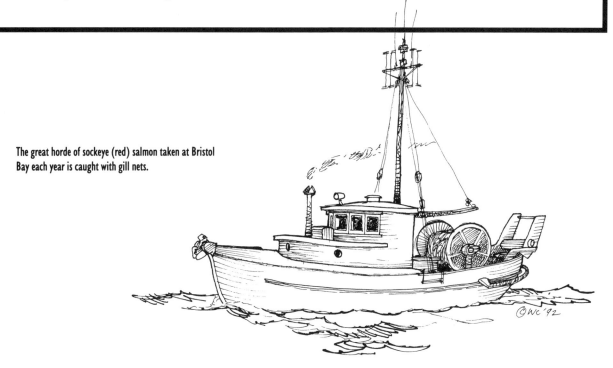

The great horde of sockeye (red) salmon taken at Bristol Bay each year is caught with gill nets.

...the wonder is always new that any sane man can be a sailor.
Ralph Waldo Emerson, *English Traits*

FACTORY PROCESSORS

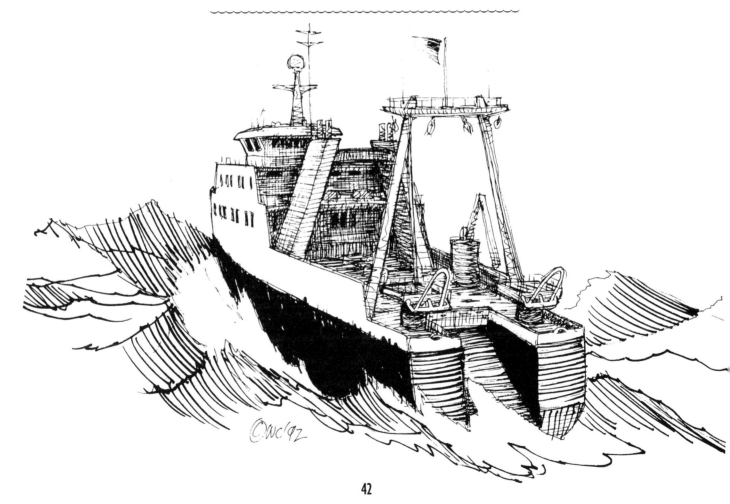

Fish processors are floating assembly lines. They are sent to fishing grounds to buy the catch from crabbers and fishing boats. Once on board, the seafood is cleaned and frozen while it is still fresh. This system allows the fishing boats to avoid frequent runs into port when their holds are full.

Although new factory processors are being built, the majority of those in the North Pacific began their lives as something else: cargo vessels or military ships. Typical is the *Courageous*, which was built as the buoy tender *Tupelo* for the Coast Guard. It was deactivated and became a processor in 1978.

The *Courageous* processes salmon, crab, Pacific cod, and other species of fish. Salmon are delivered to the *Courageous* by fishing boats under contract with the ship's owners. It works mainly along both sides of the Alaska Peninsula and out into the Bering Sea. Some crab are frozen whole; others have legs and gills removed and then are cooked and frozen. Fish are headed and gutted and then frozen and stored for offloading when the boat returns to port, usually Dutch Harbor.

More and more fish processors work as factory trawlers, meaning that they both catch and process fish and crab. While some catcher-processors use long-lines or purse seines, the *Courageous* fishes only with pots. The crab pots are modified slightly to make the entry holes a little larger when the *Courageous* is catching cod. The ship can store up to 185 tons.

Factory Processor *Courageous*

Length	180 feet
Beam	37 feet
Draft	13 feet
Propulsion	Diesel; 1,350 HP
Speed	10 to 12 knots
Construction	Steel
Crew	10 ship's crew; 22 processors

Tugboating is generally a fairly routine science, with clear margins for safe operation. Occasionally, however, the elements do not cooperate with the Captain's judgment; he gets caught with no margins left.
Dean Nichols, *Kids on the River*

HARBOR TUGS

No matter where you look along the West Coast, you will see tugs: towing barges from Los Angeles or San Francisco to Hawaii, pushing a load up the Columbia River, docking ships in San Francisco Bay, towing log booms on the Snohomish and Fraser rivers, assisting supertankers in and out of various refineries, towing tandem barges to Alaska.

Tugs come in all shapes and sizes, from the tiny one-man log broncs to the 135-foot, 7,200-horsepower units of the Crowley (Red Stack) fleet that tow the biggest loads across the Pacific Ocean.

In Seattle, tugs and the Foss Company are synonymous, not only because Foss has the largest fleet of tugs in Puget Sound but also because the company was built by local Norwegian immigrants Andrew and Thea Foss.

The Foss family arrived on Puget Sound in 1889; the rowboat-rental business they founded grew into one of the nation's largest tugboat companies. In 1969 it was merged into the Dillingham Corporation of Honolulu.

Probably the most familiar tug in Puget Sound is the *Shelley Foss* (all Foss tugs are named for members of the family, and Shelley was the granddaughter of Sidney and Barbara Foss Campbell). The *Shelley* was built in Portland's Albina Shipyard in 1970 and represented the state of the art of boat building among ship-assisting tugs.

Today she remains the best of the pre–tractor tug era of vessels. She is outfitted with inward-slanting windows that cut down on glare and with a series of viewing ports overhead, on the pilothouse's "eyebrow," that permit the captain to see tie-up lines and movements of ships. She also has twin steering nozzles, each with 88-inch propellers. Foss says the *Shelley* was so popular with ships's agents that the standard request for assist tugs was, "We need two tugs to help our ship into dock, unless the *Shelley* is assigned; then one tug will do." In her first eight years of service, she docked and undocked 12,000 ships.

When a 100-knot windstorm hit Hood Canal on February 13, 1979, the Washington State Highway Department asked Foss to send a tug to the floating bridge across Hood Canal to catch any sections of the bridge that might break loose and to move them into sheltered waters. The *Shelley* was sent out; ironically, the captain was Dan Meagher, who had been skipper of the *Carol Foss* when she towed the pontoons from Seattle to build the same bridge. As Michael Skalley wrote in his history of Foss, ". . . unfortunately, by the time the *Shelley* arrived at 10:30, the west-end pontoons were already in sheltered water—three hundred feet below the surface. The *Shelley*, unable to help the severed bridge in any way, did take the highway engineers on a waterside survey of the damage . . ."

Every tug skipper along the coast can tell a similar story because when heavy windstorms hit, ships, barges, log booms, and ferries are endangered. Tug crews stay in their boats and keep watch until the storm abates.

Life aboard a tug isn't always exciting, and most days are routine. Crews on smaller log tugs work during the daylight hours, while crews on larger harbor tugs work shifts of 15 days on and 15 days off. Crews on seagoing tugs obviously stay aboard for the duration of the trip.

Tug *Shelley Foss*

Length	90 feet
Beam	30 feet
Draft	14 feet
Propulsion	Diesel; 2 × 1,425 HP
Speed	12 knots
Construction	Steel
Crew	6

TRACTOR TUGS

46

In the early 1920s, a University of Washington aeronautical engineering professor named Dr. Frederick Kirsten took out a patent on a totally new form of marine propulsion. Unlike a standard propeller, Dr. Kirsten's model looked something like an eggbeater because it had six flat blades attached to a turntable arrangement, and the blades protruded straight down from the hull. The turntable spun, and the direction of the boat and its speed were determined by the position, or pitch, of the blades.

Dr. Kirsten installed a set of the propellers on a tugboat and filmed the boat accelerating like a sprinter out of the blocks, running full speed, spinning in 360-degree turns and then stopping almost immediately, moving sideways as well as backward. There seemed to be no movement the propellers couldn't make at any speed because the rudderless system exerted the same power in any direction.

The Boeing Company agreed that Kirsten's cycloidal propeller was the best new development for boats since the steam engine, and became a partner with Dr. Kirsten in the propeller's development, producing one or two prototypes. It was such a good system that one would think it would have become

an immediate success worldwide. Nothing like that happened in America. It was too revolutionary and customers were hard to come by, especially when the Great Depression of the 1930s descended upon the land. However, after Nazi military leaders learned of the propeller through technical journals and news stories, they put it to use during World War II on more than 100 minesweepers, two aircraft carriers, three seaplane tenders, and even four self-propelled cranes. It was ironic that Dr. Kirsten, a native of Germany who became an American patriot, had to watch the German military machine develop his invention.

Toward the end of the war, U.S. troops captured plans and parts of cycloidal propellers in Heidenheim, Germany, and these formed the basis for further research and development of the system in the U.S. after the war. A 135-foot German minesweeper was also captured in the Netherlands. No deck space could be found on homebound ships, so the Army opted to send it to America under its own power. The ship was not designed for running in the open ocean, and the crossing was rough; the skipper said that without the cycloidal propeller's added maneuverability, he might not

have made it safely. It was the first time a rudderless ship crossed the Atlantic.

The conservative maritime industry was slow to adopt the new system, and Dr. Kirsten's patent ran out. He died in 1952, disappointed that his invention never caught on. It was one of the few of his inventions that did not, though: He held more than 70 patents, including designs for electric power stations, fluorescent tubing, electric moth killers, wind tunnels, and — perhaps the most famous of them all — a tobacco pipe that is a standard in the industry.

However, times and attitudes have changed, and today the cycloidal propeller is common worldwide. Workboats of all sizes, from ships to small inland tugs and fireboats, use the system, or a near relative such as the Z-drive, which is a pair of propellers on vertical shafts placed at four locations on the boat's hull, plus steering jets. Each propeller can be turned 360 degrees, as can the steering jets.

Cycloidal propellers have many advantages. The engine doesn't need to be slowed to stop or reverse directions; with conventional propellers there is always a danger of stalling the engine while making an emergency stop or reverse. The danger of steering failure doesn't exist.

In many situations, one tractor tug can do the work of two conventional ones, such as steering a ship moving at speeds up to 10 knots. An ordinary tug doesn't have the power to turn a ship going more than 3.5 knots. Unfortunately, the cost of building the propeller and boats remains prohibitive to many tug operators.

Among those in use are four Foss tractor tugs: the *Wedell Foss*, *Henry Foss*, *Andrew Foss*, and *Arthur Foss*, all built in 1982 by Tacoma Boatbuilding. In addition, two more were ordered by Dillingham for PacTow in Long Beach, California.

A design team at Glosten Associates in Seattle spent more than two years on the project before construction began. The pilothouses have 360-degree visibility and overhead docking ports. All controls are positioned inside the pilothouse, including those for the deck winches and the 900-gallon-per-minute fire monitor on top of the wheelhouse, used for firefighting or washing the tug. Each boat normally carries a crew of six.

At this writing, Foss has announced the design and construction of a new 150-foot, 7,600-horsepower tractor tug that will be dedicated to escorting oil tankers between Port Angeles and north Puget Sound refineries.

Tractor Tugs
Wedell Foss and *Henry Foss*

Length	100 feet
Beam	36 feet
Draft	16 feet
Propulsion	Diesel; 2 × 1,500 HP
Speed	12 knots
Construction	Steel
Crew	6

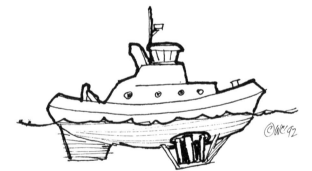

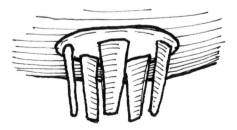

TOWBOATS

49

A linguist might call this category of boats a misnomer: Towboats actually *push* their loads. The boats are designed so the crew can see in all directions, especially ahead of the barges while pushing them from behind so they can be maneuvered into locks and through other difficult navigational hazards. The idea for these boats probably goes back to early canal and river boats, which were towed by men, horses, mules, or oxen walking along the bank. Today this type of boat is also called a pushboat, riverboat, or tug, and it works mostly on rivers and canals.

Towboats are a distant relative of the self-propelled narrow boats in the United Kingdom and the live-aboard barges you see on the Continent with the owner's automobile aboard, curtains on the portholes, and laundry flapping in the breeze.

One might wonder, on seeing a towboat and five barges cruising along the Columbia River at the speed of a family out for a stroll, why companies use barges instead of the trains and trucks that travel 10 to 15 times as fast. It is pure economics. To move 3,500 tons of grain downriver to the seagoing ships, 116 semitrailers or 35 railcars are needed—but only one towboat and one barge can do the job. The costs are considerably lower, too: about 16 cents to haul a bushel of grain on a barge, compared with 32 cents by rail and 91 cents by truck.

The Columbia/Lewis river system is 465 miles long and runs from the mouth of the Columbia to Lewiston, Idaho. The route travels through some of the world's most beautiful scenery, but it is scenery at a price for boat crews; when the wind is blowing and the weather damp and cold, it takes a lot of unpleasant work to put a tow together. The crews also have to navigate a series of locks around dams. The first dam on the downriver end is Bonneville, which has the smallest lock (although a new one, due to open in 1993, is being built). From Bonneville Dam, the tows must ease into and out of the locks at six more dams before arriving in Lewiston.

Barge traffic runs all along the Columbia River from Astoria to Lewiston. Unlike the smaller tugs towing log booms on the lower river, which must stop and tie up when the tide is running out and the river is flowing at full force, towboats pushing barges are little affected by the current.

The lock sizes limit the length of a tow to 630 feet and the width to 84 feet.

The usual tow is five barges: four side by side, with the towboat at the rear and the fifth barge alongside the towboat, or "on its hip," as boatmen say. This load is called a lockage. It isn't much by Mississippi River standards, where locks are much larger. There tows can stretch for a quarter mile, and towboats have three times the power of those on the Columbia River.

The towboats generally have a crew of four, or sometimes five for longer runs: a captain, a deckhand, junior and senior crew, and an engineer. They usually work 15 days on and 15 days off. In the past the boats had a full-time cook, but now that duty is assigned to one of the deckhands.

As towboats have become more efficient, so have barges. Companies now have barges that are self-unloading and refrigerated. Tidewater, which was the first barge line to run on a regular schedule on the Columbia, was also the first to use self-unloading barges for grain. These barges have a V-shaped bottom with augers along the notch of the V that continually move the grain to the marine leg, a conveyer with a series of small buckets on shore. Another company, Brix Maritime, recently built a refrigerated barge to ship prepared foods, mostly

The ocean tug is exemplified by Crowley Maritime's 135-foot, 7,200 horsepower, twin-screw Invader class tugs. These tugs tow tandem 400-foot rail barges between Seattle and Whittier, Alaska year-round. They also tow freight barges between the West Coast and Hawaii.

frozen potato products — french fries and hash browns—from Idaho, eastern Washington, and Oregon.

It takes an average of 55 hours to make a one-way trip between Portland and Lewiston. With nearly all of the journey between Portland–Vancouver and Lewiston made on slack water behind the series of dams, most of the danger of navigating the Columbia River has been removed. In the old days of barging, the crews were often in danger of stacking a load of barges on rocks, most of which now are submerged. These rocks still have names, some in honor of the skippers who ran into them. Before the dams were built, the Snake River was especially difficult to steer because it ran so fast and was so crooked. One story, perhaps apocryphal,

involved the skipper who stacked up his barges on a rock where he had never had problems before. When he had to explain himself, he said there was a barn nearby, and for years he had used it as a navigational aid; when he could see a tree on the far side through the open doors, he made his turn. On the day of his disaster, somebody closed one of the doors.

Despite the taming of the rivers, life on the towboats and barges is still challenging. The Columbia Gorge is the only slot in the Cascade Range through which weather can move through unobstructed, so it has some of the strongest winds in the Northwest (which also makes it a prime area for the windsurfers who flit back and forth among the towboats and barges like water bugs). The gorge also has some of the

region's worst weather, and ice is often a problem. During the gorge's frequent storms, the towboat deckhands use double tie-downs, called storm gear, to lash the cargo. This work should be completed before they get under way because it is very difficult to make adjustments once the tow is moving through heavy winds and whipping water.

Towboat *Sundial*

Length	92 feet
Beam	30 feet
Draft	12 feet 6 inches
Propulsion	Diesel; 2 × 1,500 HP
Speed	5 to 7 knots under tow
Construction	Steel
Crew	4 or 5

SALVAGE TUGS

The *Arctic Salvor*, owned by Crowley Maritime Corporation of San Francisco, California, is one of the largest and most versatile tugs in the world. It is used to raise sunken vessels, remove wrecks, perform underwater repairs, and refloat grounded ships. The most powerful salvage tug on the West Coast, it has more line pull (pulling power) for freeing grounded vessels than any other salvage vessel in the United States. The pulling power is developed by its anchor system combined with its winches.

The 213-foot-long tug is equipped with a helicopter pad, a 35-ton crane, a 21-foot workboat, a 16-foot skiff, a decompression chamber, two diving compressors, four winches capable of hauling 300,000 pounds, four welding machines, two fire-fighting monitors, and accommodations for 25 (a salvage team of 17 plus the regular operating crew of 8). In addition to the captain, mate, engineers, and deckhands, two divers are on board at all times. With a fuel capacity of over 81,000 gallons, the *Arctic Salvor* has a cruising range of 30 days.

Because the tug is an emergency vessel, it sometimes lies in port for weeks or months at a time. Occasionally it serves as a support vessel for Crowley projects, such as delivering oil-field supplies to Prudhoe Bay, Alaska. During the *Exxon Valdez* oil spill cleanup, the tug was used as a supply vessel, with the stipulation that if a marine emergency occurred, it would drop whatever it was doing and head for the emergency.

Perhaps its most visible role came in November 1990, when, during high winds, the original Interstate 90 floating bridge that connected Seattle and Mercer Island began sinking; the *Arctic Salvor* was called upon to hold a newly built bridge steady after some of its anchor cables were severed when the old bridge sank.

The tug, originally a support vessel named the *Manatee*, was built in 1970 for use in the Caribbean. Crowley Maritime acquired it and in 1980 remodeled it into a salvage tug. Seattle is its home base.

Salvage Tug *Arctic Salvor*

Length	213 feet
Beam	53 feet
Draft	14 feet
Propulsion	Diesel; 2 × 1,150 HP
Speed	12 knots
Construction	Steel
Crew	8 for operations; 17 for salvage

BARGES

Barges come in many sizes, ranging from 100 to more than 400 feet in length. They are made of steel and are of solid construction. They can haul an enormous load— 12,000 tons and more—and are designed and built as specialized carriers or simply in flat-deck configurations that can be adapted to various cargoes. Fuel barges, for example, can haul more than one million gallons at a time and still have enough freeboard (the surface between the deck and waterline) left to carry a few containers on top of the deck. These fuel barges are divided into five or six separate tanks.

Barges average 6 to 8 knots while under tow, which means it takes about five days to haul a load from Seattle to Sitka, Alaska. During the summer months, tugs often tow two barges in tandem through the Inside Passage. Tugs need engines of at least 3,500 horsepower and as much as 5,000 horsepower to pull a tandem of 300-foot barges.

Some barges look top-heavy during the summer months because they have 8-foot-tall containers stacked five high. Loads are limited to four high during the stormy winter months, but after March, when the weather generally improves, loads will return to five layers high.

The containers are held together with cones on each corner that fit into holes in the container above, so that the containers almost snap together. Forklifts load the barges, and when the load is complete, it is secured with a web of lashing chain and turnbuckles to prevent shifting and toppling.

One coastal operation is Samson Tug & Barge. The company operates several tugs and barges and specializes in the Alaska market. Their loads going north can be anything from clothing and food to privately owned automobiles and household goods. In 1992, it cost about $900 to ship a car in a container from Seattle to Alaska. Samson also hauls all kinds of liquid fuel—gasoline, diesel, jet fuel, and bunker oil. When the barges return to Seattle, they often carry fresh fish in refrigerated containers or canned salmon.

A familiar sight in British Columbia is the chip barge, with its high, open box heaped with wood chips for delivery to the pulp mills. You might also see very large log barges outfitted with cranes and carrying their own log broncs, which load logs from the water at remote logging sites and literally dump the entire 15,000-ton load at their destination.

Other duties assigned to barges include deliveries of lumber and wood products from the Northwest and British Columbia to California and Hawaii, newsprint from British Columbia to San Francisco and Los Angeles, salt from California and Mexico to the caustic plants in the Northwest, and petroleum products to the harbors all along the Pacific Coast. You name it, there is a barge and tug to do the job.

When a barge is being towed, the tug will show two masthead lights in a vertical line if the towing cable is less than 656 feet long. If it is longer, the tug must show three lights on its mast in a vertical line. It must also display a stern light, a towing light above the stern light, and the diamond shape—a black symbol attached to a halyard about halfway up the mast.

Barges in tow to Prudhoe Bay, Alaska,
with icebreaker escort.

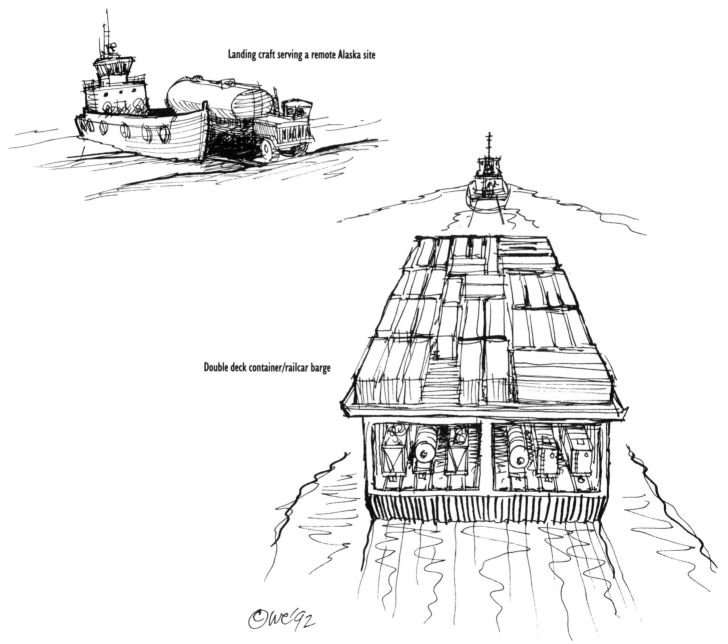

Landing craft serving a remote Alaska site

Double deck container/railcar barge

Owe'92

57

Bulk urea barge with northbound deck load

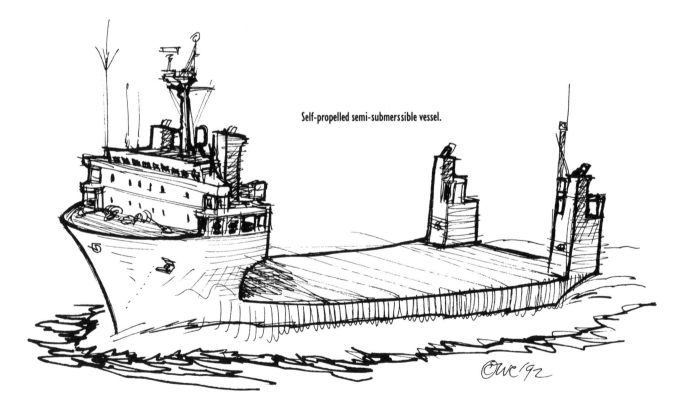

Self-propelled semi-submerssible vessel.

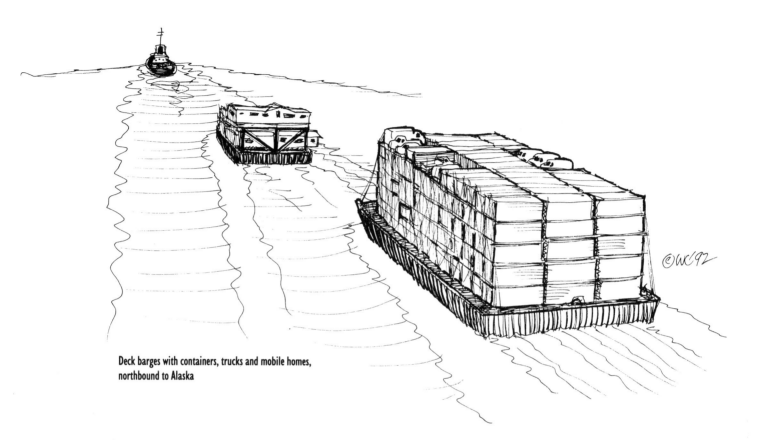

Deck barges with containers, trucks and mobile homes,
northbound to Alaska

Fuel delivery by barge

Shallow draft tugs pushing a barge

In fine weather, particularly on the passage to North Vancouver, it was sheer pleasure to view the wonderful skyline, the snow-capped Lions and the majestic beauty of the North Shore mountains and I often thought to myself, "Fancy getting paid for doing this!" There were, of course, other times and other weather conditions when the monthly stipend seemed a bit inadequate. Captain James Barr, Ferry Across the Harbor

FERRIES AND PASSENGER BOATS

NORTHWEST FERRIES

©WC'92

British Columbia's fleet of ferries is one of the largest in the world in terms of total route miles (918) and the number of miles its passengers travel each year. The number of passengers riding these ferries annually recently surpassed the totals for Washington's ferry system. During the 1991–92 season, the Canadian fleet carried 19.7 million passengers and 7.7 million vehicles compared with the Washington fleet's 12.8 million passengers and 9.6 million vehicles. This may seem like a lot of traffic, but neither can approach the number of passengers carried by the Hong Kong Star ferry system: more than 12 million passengers a month!

British Columbia, with its thousands of miles of coastline between Vancouver, Victoria, and Prince Rupert, supports a fleet of 40 vessels — nearly twice Washington's 25 vessels, which include three passenger-only ferries.

Unlike many of their British Columbia counterparts, which look more like cruise ships than ferries, the Washington vessels have open car decks. When you see one sailing directly into the sunset with a vast, open vehicle area, it looks slightly vulnerable. Don't be fooled; in spite of an occasional mishap — losing a sports car off a ramp, running aground on a mud flat, or even playing bump-and-run with each other — the ferries are as durable and safe as a Boeing 747.

The ferry system is especially proud of its Jumbo Class vessels — the *Spokane* and *Walla Walla* — because they have had the best service records in the fleet. They have performed so well that the next generation of ferries, expected to be built by the mid-1990s, will be almost identical to the *Spokane* and *Walla Walla*.

The largest B.C. ferries enclose their car decks with doors because many of their long routes are subject to bad weather. In addition, the B.C. ferries's passenger areas have more amenities, including ship-to-shore phones, newsstands, cocktail lounges, and full meal service.

Beginning at the northern reaches of the British Columbia coast, ferries run between Prince Rupert on the mainland and the Queen Charlotte Islands, a 93-mile trip, and from Prince Rupert via the Inside Passage to Port Hardy, the system's longest run at 274 miles. Other ferries crisscross between Vancouver Island and the mainland, with the busiest routes being the mainland–Victoria-area routes from Vancouver (Horseshoe Bay) and Tsawwassen near the U.S. border.

Washington's ferries don't offer as many diversions because only in the San Juan Islands are passengers aboard more than a hour. The longest of all the Washington ferry runs is between Anacortes, Washington and Sidney, British Columbia, on Vancouver Island; it takes about three hours.

Washington's six largest ferries — *Spokane, Walla Walla, Hyak, Kaleetan, Yakima*, and *Elwha* — sail with a crew of 14. On the largest, the *Spokane* and *Walla Walla*, the crew comprises the master, chief and second mates, four able-bodied seamen, three ordinary seamen, a chief and assistant engineer, and two oilers. On the other four, slightly smaller vessels, the second mate is replaced by an additional ordinary seaman.

The crew size diminishes with the vessel size; on the smallest of them all — the *Olympic* and *Hiyu* — the crew consists of a master, two able-bodied seamen, an engineer, and an oiler.

Each crew member has specific jobs to perform in port and while under way. The master or captain is responsible for the entire vessel. The first mate, who might hold a master's license, assists the captain. You will see the second mate at the end of the car deck directing traffic because he or she is in charge of loading and unloading.

The bosun and deckhands help direct cars, handle lines at the dock, act as lookouts, patrol the vessel for safety hazards, and clean the ship each time it docks.

The engineers monitor the systems on the newer vessels, while on older ones they control the engine speed and direction by following orders from the captain. The oilers get their title from the old days, when they patrolled the engine room with oil cans making sure oil cups were full. They still patrol the engine room (but without the oil cans, because nearly all of today's engines have sealed bearings), and they assist the engineers in maintenance.

The B.C. ferries's crews are almost identical. On the 426-foot *Queen of Esquimalt*, for example, the crew totals 13, including the master, chief officer, second officer, and six ordinary seamen above decks. In the engine room are the chief engineer, second engineer, junior engineer, and an oiler.

Washington ferries are divided into several size classes. The specification tables give information on the largest and smallest of these. The Jumbo Class *Spokane* and *Walla Walla* each can carry 206 cars and 2,000 passengers. In comparison, the 150-foot *Hiyu* transports 40 cars and 200 passengers.

The British Columbia fleet doesn't break down into specific classes, as do the Washington ferries, because the

Washington State Ferry Whistles

One long and two short blasts	Approaching dock
One long blast	Departing dock
One short blast	Turning right
Two short blasts	Turning left
Three short blasts	Engine reversed
Four or more short blasts	Danger

(Usually directed at pleasure boats that have challenged ferry's right of way.)

needs of the fleet are so diverse. It needs ferries for the busy runs between the lower end of Vancouver Island and the Vancouver area, for a host of shorter runs with light traffic, and for the long runs to Prince Rupert and across Hecate Strait to the Queen Charlotte Islands. However, the fleet does operate two groups of large ferries that are quite similar. The six C-Class Jumbos measure 129.97 meters (426 feet); the seven Cowichan Class vessels measure 139.97 meters (457 feet).

The 129.97-meter group includes the *Queen of Burnaby, Queen of Esquimalt, Queen of New Westminster, Queen of Saanich, Queen of Vancouver*, and *Queen of Victoria*. Another vessel, the *Queen of New Westminster*, recently joined this fleet at 129.96 meters, an inch shorter than the others. The C-Class Jumbos can carry 295 to 362 cars and 1,360 to 1,466 passengers. The larger Cowichan Class transports up to 362 cars and 1,466 passengers.

Washington State Ferries, Jumbo Class *Spokane* and *Walla Walla*

Length...440 feet
Beam..87 feet
Draft ....18 feet
Propulsion ....4 diesel generators; 11,500 HP
8,500 HP electric motor at each end
Speed..18 knots
Construction ....Steel

Washington State Ferry *Hiyu*

Length ....150 feet
Beam..63 feet
Draft..11 feet
Propulsion ....Diesel; 2
Speed..10 knots
Construction ....Steel

British Columbia Ferries, Cowichan Class

Length...460 feet
Beam..90 feet
Draft ....15 feet
Propulsion..................................Diesel; 11,840 HP
Speed..19 knots
Construction ....Steel

British Columbia Ferries, C-Class Jumbo (Victoria Class)

Length...426 feet
Beam..80 feet
Draft ....13 to 15 feet
Propulsion ....Diesel; 6,000 to 11,840 HP
Speed...16 to 19 knots
Construction ....Steel

Queen of Oak Bay, a B.C. Cowichan class ferry

Washington State Ferries

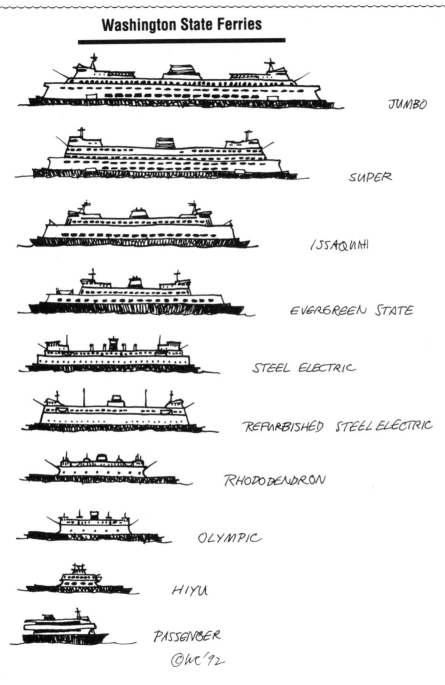

JUMBO

SUPER

ISSAQUAH

EVERGREEN STATE

STEEL ELECTRIC

REFURBISHED STEEL ELECTRIC

RHODODENDRON

OLYMPIC

HIYU

PASSENGER
©WC '92

A LITTLE HISTORY

The two largest ferry systems in North America are almost blood kin: Both are second-generation services founded by the same man, Alexander Marshall Peabody, whose family owned the Puget Sound Navigation Company. He founded the Black Ball Line, a fleet of passenger ferries in both British Columbia and Washington, in 1928. The current provincial and state ferry systems both owe their origins to their respective governments, which nudged, forced, and finally bought out Peabody.

Washington's legislature had been casting covetous eyes on Black Ball for a long time because it rankled many politicians to have a private company controlling so much of the state's transportation system. Peabody, of course, wasn't a complete victim in the dispute, which continued for several years, because his business methods did not always put the welfare

The steam-powered *San Mateo* ferried passengers and cars in San Francisco Bay before heading north and joining the Black Ball fleet in the 1940s.

© WC'92

of citizens first. Consequently, the legislature and governor's office found a number of ways to make it almost impossible for Peabody to continue his business. Finally, at the end of 1950, the state bought him out for $5 million. The deal included 16 ferries, 20 terminals, other equipment, and access roads on Hood Canal. Peabody kept five ferries and the Seattle–Port Angeles–Victoria route.

In British Columbia, labor disputes and work stoppages drove the government to buy Peabody's company.

In 1958, Premier W. A. C. Bennett announced that the provincial government was going into the ferry business, and he meant it. At his urging, the government bought Black Ball's remaining five-vessel fleet of ferries and terminals for $6.8 million. Of Peabody's whole private system, which once ranged from the lower end of Puget Sound to the upper reaches of Vancouver Island, only the Port Angeles–Victoria ferry *Coho* remains in service today.

The streamlined *Kalakala*, a former Washington State ferry, was known locally as the Silver Slug. The boat is now used as a fish processing plant in Alaska.

FERRY CREWS

Quartermaster: This is an able-bodied seaman (AB) with a lot of experience in the system and in steering the vessels. The quartermaster follows all rudder commands given by the mate or master and is responsible for checking all running lights, radar, and radios. Many ferries still have the traditional spoked wheels, but the trend is toward steering levers that give better control of the rudders. The quartermaster uses radar and a compass for steering and also uses the guidon for steering by sight. The guidon is the pole that protrudes at about a 45-degree angle from below the pilothouse at each end of the vessel. The quartermaster can steer a straight course by keeping the tip of the guidon on a landmark.

Lookout: This is usually an AB who is in the pilothouse during darkness to help watch for hazards that radar might not detect.

Witness: This is usually an ordinary seaman (OS) who comes to the bridge during landings as an additional set of eyes to give tachometer and other instrument readings to the master or mate, who is sometimes unable to watch.

Wing Person: This is an AB who works on the auto deck on both sides of the vessel. The newest wing person always works on the north end of the vessel because it is colder (R.H.I.P.—Rank Has Its Privileges).

Tunnel Person: This OS works in the center of the vessel directing traffic and making sure that the lead vehicles are blocked before departure and unblocked on arrival.

Tail Gunner: The quartermaster "tail-guns" from the offshore pilothouse on the older vessels during arrivals, signaling the master with a buzzer system: One buzz means "hard right," and two mean "hard left." Three buzzes mean "center the rudder." This is the only method the master has of operating the bow rudder on older vessels during landings. Newer and refurbished vessels have eliminated the need for tail gunners.

Fog Lookout: This person is stationed "as far forward and as close to the water as possible" during periods of fog and limited visibility. He or she listens for outboard motors on craft too small for the radar to pick up, foghorns, and other sounds.

Car Deck Patrol: This is usually an AB who roams the car deck during the crossing, checking for smokers (smoking is illegal on the car deck because of fire hazard) or anything out of the ordinary, and reports to the master several times during the trip to let him know all is well.

Cabin Person: This person does whatever is necessary to keep the cabin clean and to assist passengers.

A **purser** is added to Washington ferries's crew on the international route between Anacortes, Washington, and Sidney, British Columbia. **Customs officers** are also usually aboard these runs.

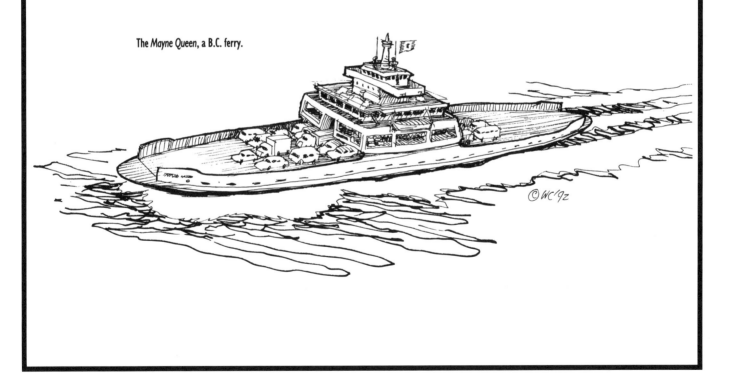

The *Mayne Queen*, a B.C. ferry.

FERRY FOLKLORE

In the British Columbia fleet, a story is told about a commuter at Departure Bay who always waited until the last possible minute to kiss his wife goodbye and then would make a mad dash for the ferry, often having to jump the last few feet. One day when he made his run, the gap between dock and ferry was wider than usual, but he threw his briefcase aboard and successfully made the leap.

"Well done, sir," said a seaman with a grin, "but we are just arriving."

Because commuting by ferry can be a daily event, criticisms of the ferry systems are frequently brandished by the people who rely most heavily on them, especially residents of the small islands of Washington and between Vancouver Island and the Canadian mainland. Many of these people have a love-hate relationship with the ferry system, but if you really want a fight on your hands, try suggesting to them that bridges be built to their islands so they won't have to depend on the ferries!

Ferries run back and forth without turning around, because if they did, all the cars and trucks would have to back off. Consequently, regular passengers become accustomed to this and, being creatures of habit, board the ferry, get their cup of coffee and doughnut, head for their favorite place to sit — fourth booth from the bow, port side — and read the morning paper or go over work projects until the ferry lands. Commuters will do this for years.

Occasionally the ferry captain will have a sense of humor, especially on April 1, and will start the day off with the ferry reversed. The crew is treated to the spectacle of passengers milling around like confused cattle, looking for their seats. Most take it in stride, but there are always a few who get very grouchy when faced with something unexpected.

NOMENCLATURE

Here's a partial list of the Washington ferry names and what they mean in the original Native American languages common around Puget Sound when Europeans arrived.

Chelan: A tribe and lake

Elwha: Clallam for elk

Hiyu: Chinook for plenty or much

Hyak: Chinook for fast or speedy

Illahee: Chinook for land, place, or location

Issaquah: A city; the origin of the word is uncertain

Kaleetan: Chinook for arrow

Kathlamet: A tribe along the lower Columbia River

Kitsap: A sub-chief under Chief Sealth of the Suquamish tribe

Kittitas: A central Washington tribe

Klahowya: Chinook for greetings of welcome

Klickitat: A tribe from central Washington along the Columbia River

Nisqually: A tribe at the mouth of the Nisqually River

Quinault: A tribe

Sealth: The Suquamish chief for whom Seattle was named

Spokane: A tribe

It was the British, the apostles of rose gardens and high tea, who nicknamed [Victoria] "England of the Pacific,"
and sent boatloads of pipe-smoking, tweed-wearing, Queen-loving, tea-drinking gentlemen here to settle it.
Timothy Egan, *The Good Rain*

FERRIES AND PASSENGER BOATS

VICTORIA CLIPPER

High-speed catamarans are becoming more prevalent as passenger-only ferries throughout the world because they are so stable, spacious, and fast. As the Polynesians learned centuries ago, two hulls are better than one for safety—it is almost impossible to flip a two-hulled vessel, and they give a better ride because they are much less susceptible to rolling. They are faster for much the same reason; because their weight is distributed over a larger area, they don't draw as much water as a monohull of similar size.

The *Victoria Clipper* has been on the run between Seattle and Victoria, B.C., since 1985. The route has been so successful that two additional ships were built, one in 1989 and the other in 1990, after the venerable queen of the run, the steamship *Princess Marguerite*, was retired.

Owned by Clipper Navigation, a Seattle company, the boats are also used for dinner cruises, and during the summer other towns are sometimes added to the schedule as traffic demands — Port Townsend, Friday Harbor, and LaConner. The *Victoria Clipper III* is outfitted with special racks for bicycles and kayaks. The company has also been licensed to carry small packages and cargo on its routes.

Nichols Brothers of Whidbey Island became involved in catamarans for passenger service when the yard built a catamaran to haul passengers from Seattle to a resort on Hood Canal. This led to a licensing agreement with International Catamarans, Ltd., and Nichols then built catamarans for the Red and White fleet of commuter boats on San Francisco Bay as well as the *Victoria Clippers*. The largest of the Nichols-built fleet is the *Catalina Flyer*, which carries up to 600 passengers at 30 knots between Balboa and Catalina Island, California.

The specifications table shows information for the *Victoria Clipper III*, which can carry 2,390 passengers. The 127-foot *Clipper I* and the 97-foot *Clipper II* carry 300 and 285 passengers, respectively.

Victoria Clipper

Length	114 feet
Beam	28 feet
Draft	3 feet
Propulsion	Diesel; 2 × 1,600 HP
Speed	25 knots
Construction	Aluminum
Crew	2 to 3 on bridge

The day was breaking as we crossed the ferry; the fog was rising over the cstied hills of San Francisco; the bay was perfect—
not a ripple, scarce a stain, upon its blue expanse; everything was waiting, breathless, for the sun.
Robert Louis Stevenson, Arriving in San Francisco

SAN FRANCISCO BAY FERRIES

A San Francisco Bay catamaran

Before the Golden Gate Bridge opened in 1937, the world's largest ferry fleet—more than 50 vessels—crisscrossed San Francisco Bay to the towns north and east of the city. This giant fleet included sternwheelers, sidewheelers, and the more mundane but efficient propeller-driven boats. Passenger traffic diminished when the San Francisco–Oakland Bay Bridge opened in 1936 and, a year later, virtually stopped when the Golden Gate Bridge was completed.

Ferry traffic didn't resume for nearly 50 years, but gradually a fleet of passenger-only ferries returned as the cities around San Francisco Bay grew to the point that automobile traffic and parking in the city were almost intolerable.

Today several companies run scheduled passenger ferries from the Ferry Building at the foot of Market Street and Piers 41 and 43½. They go to Sausalito, Tiburon, Larkspur, Angel Island, Vallejo, Oakland, and Alameda. Two of the major companies are Golden Gate Ferries and the Red and White Fleet. They operate standard monohull vessels as well as large catamarans. Golden Gate has three almost identical 750-passenger ferries named the *Marin*, *Sonoma*, and *San Francisco*. They went into service between December 1976 and September 1977. They carry a crew of four.

San Francisco Bay Ferries
Marin, *Sonoma*, and *San Francisco*

Length	169 feet
Beam	34 feet
Draft	6 feet
Propulsion	Diesel; 2 × 1,570 HP
Speed	20 knots
Construction	Aluminum
Crew	4

We were very tired, we were very merry—We had gone back and forth all night on the ferry.
Edna St. Vincent Millay, Recuerdo

FERRIES AND PASSENGER BOATS

NICKEL SNATCHERS

More than any of the thousands of Navy ships that cruised in and out of San Diego's harbor, the lowly passenger ferries the sailors called "nickel snatchers" were the symbol of San Diego from the 1930s to the 1960s.

Sailors stationed on North Island Naval Air Station, or whose ships were moored there, used these sturdy ferries that ran from the foot of Broadway across to the island. They were called nickel snatchers because for 37 years, it cost only a nickel to ride them. When rising expenses forced the owners to increase the fare in 1955 to a dime, sailors grumbled and began calling the ferries the "dime grabbers."

San Diego Harbor Excursions owned at least seven of the red, white, and blue vessels during their heyday. Among them were the *Glorietta*, which now is a gift shop with no engine, the *Monterey*, the *Silver Gate*, the *Ramona*, the *Point Loma*, the *Del Mar*, and the *Juanita*.

The demise of nickel snatchers came swiftly after the long, curving Coronado Toll Bridge was built from the mainland to Coronado in 1969. The *Silver Gate*, built in 1940 in San Diego, recently went back into service carrying passengers and bicycles between Coronado and San Diego. Obviously, the days of the five-cent fare are gone forever. At this writing, the 12-minute crossing costs $2 per passenger and 60 cents for bicycles.

Nickel Snatcher
Silver Gate

Length	58.5 feet
Beam	21.3 feet
Draft	7 feet
Propulsion	Diesel; 2 × 150 HP
Speed	10 to 12 knots
Construction	Wood
Crew	3

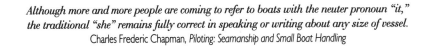

FERRIES AND PASSENGER BOATS

VIRGINIA V

During the half century between Washington's statehood and World War II, very few towns along Puget Sound were served by highways or railroads. The few roads that did exist were usually dirt, which meant that at least half of the time they were not much more than parallel mud puddles. Thus, the inland sea literally swarmed with boats that hauled passengers, mail, and cargo. So many boats of all descriptions littered the waterways that people said they grew like mosquitoes on a pond, and these boats became known as the Mosquito Fleet.

The *Virginia V* (say "five," not "Vee") is the last steamer of this large fleet and is still going strong. As her number indicates, the *Virginia V* was the fifth (and final) boat named Virginia that the West Pass Transportation Company built. (The boats were named after Virginia Merrill, daughter of a local timber baron.) The company, owned by Nels

G. Christinsen and his sons Nels C., Vern, and Andrew, was headquartered at Lisabeula on the west side of Vashon Island. Their boats operated the 13-stop run between Seattle and Tacoma along the Kitsap side of Puget Sound, through Colvos Passage (or West Pass) between Vashon Island and the mainland. Only two of the towns from that era remain somewhat intact, Olalla and Fragaria.

The *Virginia V* was built in the winter of 1921–22 at Matt Anderson's boatyard at the now-extinct town of Maplewood on the Kitsap mainland near Olalla. No plans were drawn; Christinsen told Anderson to follow the designs of two previous boats he had built, so they copied the superstructure of *Vashon II* and the hull of *Virginia III*. The boat is still run today on her original 400-horsepower steam engine built in 1898. When she was launched, the *Virginia V* was christened with a bottle of water from Lisabeula Creek. One of her duties was hauling Camp Fire Girls to their camp

on Vashon Island, a charter the boat continued to run for several decades.

A former crew member of the boat, Gordon Grant, once described a typical day aboard the boat as beginning at 7:00 A.M., when the *Virginia V* departed from Tacoma for Seattle. She arrived in Seattle at about 9:45 A.M., after making several stops along West Pass. Not all 13 stops were made each trip—only those that had a flag out. At about 11:00 A.M. she left Seattle for Tacoma and sailed nonstop through the East Pass to arrive at Tacoma at about 1:15 P.M. She left Tacoma again at 2:00 P.M., arrived in Seattle at about 4:15 P.M., and left for the last trip of the day to Tacoma at 5:00 P.M. She logged about 46,000 miles a year until 1939.

In 1940 and 1941, she was a troop ship, transporting men from the 248th Coast Artillery between forts Worden, Casey, and Flagler in Puget Sound.

Her career faltered during the rest of

the war. She was taken to the Columbia River to run between Astoria and Portland, Oregon. The owners went broke, and she was sold by the U.S. marshal. New owners brought her back to Puget Sound and began the West Pass run again. But after the war, business declined, and like the entire Mosquito Fleet, the *Virginia V* was relegated to the transportation backwaters when the state of Washington decided in 1950 to invest in its own ferry fleet as an extension of the state highway system. She was used almost exclusively for excursions during the next three decades.

Virginia V

Length	125 feet
Beam	24 feet
Draft	11 feet
Propulsion	Steam engine: triple expansion 400 horsepower 200 psi
Speed	14 knots top speed, cruises at 8 to 10 knots
Construction	Douglas fir; frames, 8-inch square, 22-inch spacing; planks, 3 inches thick; deck beams, 5 × 6 inches, 25-inch spacing
Crew	7 (Licensed captain, mate, engineer, fireman, and 3 deckhands)

During this time, she went through a succession of owners until the Virginia V Foundation, formed in 1976, bought her in 1979 with state and federal grants and matching funds from supporters.

Today the boat continues to be chartered to private parties, carrying up to 328 passengers. She is operated in much the same manner as she was during her heyday on the Sound because grandfather clauses waive many Coast Guard regulations that apply to new boats—provided the *Virginia V* is in good working condition.

SAFETY WORKBOATS

FIREBOATS

The traditional welcome for a special ship entering a harbor is to send out a fireboat to accompany it into port, pumps arcing fountains of water, creating rainbows in the sunlight. This is the best of circumstances for a fireboat, including the Seattle Fire Department's newest boat, the *Chief Seattle*, which is typical of a West Coast fireboat.

The 96-foot vessel was built by Nichols Brothers of Whidbey Island, Washington, for the much more serious business of fighting fires, performing rescues, and providing emergency medical services along Seattle's waterfront.

The *Chief Seattle* has been in service since 1985 and has an impressive inventory of tools and equipment built into it. Each of the three engines produces 1,050 horsepower, and each can simultaneously provide power to the three 45-inch, fixed-pitch propellers and to the 2,500-gallons-per-minute seawater pumps. The boat can remain stationary while pumping 100 percent of its pump capacity dead ahead, as well as 50 percent of its broadside capacity.

A work-and-rescue skiff is cradled on a water-level platform on the stern and is accessible via an easy slide-on, slide-off ramp. The platform can also be used for rescue work.

The fireboat is equipped with six nozzles, which fire fighters call "monitors." The tower nozzle can be elevated 45 feet above the water and operated by remote control from both inside and outside the pilothouse. It looks like a small cannon and can pump 6,000 gallons of water or 500 gallons of fire-extinguishing foam per minute. A pair of 2,000-gallons-per-minute monitors, fitted on both port and starboard sides of the waterline at the bow, can be used for fire fighting or as maneuvering thrusters. Each side has seven 3½-inch hose ports and one 2½-inch port equipped with an automatic foam system for hand-held foam lines. Two other monitors, with a capacity of 2,500 gallons per minute, are at the aft end of the bridge deck, and still another manually operated monitor, with a capacity of more than 4,400 gallons per minute, is on the bow.

In order for crew members to concentrate on fire fighting, the *Chief Seattle* has a fully automated engine room, and all functions are monitored and controlled from the pilothouse; no crew member needs to be in the engine room.

A remote station on the aft end of the bridge deck allows the skipper to operate the boat from there because rescues are usually conducted from the stern.

The 1,500 gallons of diesel fuel the *Chief Seattle* carries is enough for it to run at full speed for an hour and then pump to capacity for 12 hours while holding itself in position with its triple screws, triple rudders, and fore and aft maneuvering jets.

In addition, the fireboat has an emergency medical services room where two severe-trauma patients can be treated at the same time.

The boat is so automated that it requires a crew of only four, who work shifts of 24 hours on and 24 hours off.

Fireboat *Chief Seattle*

Length	96 feet
Beam	23 feet
Draft	7 feet
Propulsion	Diesel; 3 × 1,050 HP
Speed	26 knots
Construction	Welded aluminum
Crew	4

OIL SPILL RECOVERY VESSELS

Oil spill recovery vessels were created by an act of Congress in the 1960s, in response to some massive oil spills. With public pressure on, Congress told the Coast Guard to develop marine oil-recovery systems. The Coast Guard sent out requests for proposals, and a Martin Marietta Company team, led by Dr. J. L. McGrew, developed what the scientists called "flat sheets of open-celled, fully-reticulated polyurethane foam, fabricated into a moving conveyor belt."

McGrew's team didn't invent the foam. Credit for that goes to Scott Paper Company, which developed it for use in aircraft and rocket fuel tanks to keep the liquid fuel from sloshing around in flight and in zero gravity. To make the foam more suitable for cleaning up oil spills, the Martin Marietta team added large pores to the material that permit water but not oil to pass through.

A conveyor belt made of this material is positioned with its front end beneath the surface of the water and the other end hanging over into the recovery vessel. The belt picks up the oil and debris and carries it into the boat, where a scraper and squeeze roller remove it. The system was named the Filterbelt. In 1972, MARCO of Seattle purchased the technology.

MARCO, Munson, and other boat builders began a family of vessels and unmanned boats called skimmers, some using their own designs and others in response to specific requests or specialized needs of government and industrial customers.

The smallest skimmers are towed alongside a boat. A V-boom in front of each skimmer forces the oil onto the 48-inch-wide Filterbelt. One skimmer, the Class XIV, can recover 24,000 barrels (one million gallons) in just over two days. This equates to 500 barrels an hour.

Several manned oil spill recovery vessels are in operation along the West Coast. Most of them are built for speed, so they can get to a spill before it spreads. One such boat, the tractor oil recovery (TOR) vessel from MARCO, is 75 feet long and retrieves 900 gallons per minute. The TOR can store 500 barrels of recovered oil.

Schematic of Class XIV skimmer and Voss mast and spar system

Oil Spill Recovery Vessel, Class XIV Skimmer

Length	19 feet
Beam	9 feet
Draft	3 feet
Propulsion	None
Speed	Towed
Construction	Aluminum
Crew	Unmanned

Oil Spill Recovery Vessel, Tractor Oil Recovery (TOR) Vessel

Length	75 feet
Beam	21 feet
Draft	9 feet
Propulsion	Diesel; 600 HP with Z-drive; stern thruster 80 HP
Construction	Aluminum
Crew	3

CANADIAN RESCUE BOATS

The Canadians's most exotic rescue vessels are the three Hovercrafts, two in service at Vancouver International Airport and the other at Parksville on Vancouver Island. These air-cushion vehicles are used in places where normal boats cannot operate effectively — on mud flats and in areas that have powerful tidal rapids and whirlpools. Hovercrafts, used extensively in Europe but less so in North America, ride on a cushion of air generated by powerful fans so that the boats are truly amphibious and can run across tide flats and rapids with ease. Hovercrafts have a range of 10 hours. They have a three-person crew: a captain, a navigator, and a search-and-rescue specialist with medical training.

More familiar are the three 12.4-meter (33-foot) rescue boats *Osprey*, *Mallard*, and *Skua*, which operate out of Kitsilano, Powell River, and Bamfield. These boats have a crew of three and perform a series of chores in addition to search-and-rescue missions.

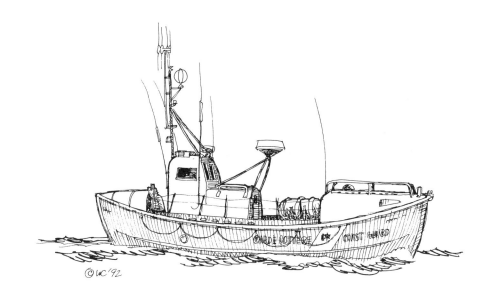

Canadian Coast Guard Hovercraft

Length	49 feet
Beam	23 feet
Draft	0
Propulsion	Rolls-Royce Gnome gas turbine; 1,100 HP
Speed	60 knots top speed, cruises at 40 knots
Construction	Fiberglass hull with flexible skirts
Crew	3

Canadian Coast Guard Search and Rescue Boat

Length	33 feet
Beam	14 feet
Draft	4 feet
Propulsion	Diesel; 2 × 400 HP
Speed	26 knots top speed, cruises at 22 knots
Crew	3

A sentimental favorite is the old *Banfield* lifeboat. (Yes, it is *Banfield* rather than *Bamfield*, where it is stationed.) The wooden-hulled vessel continues to be well-maintained by the Coast Guard, even though it is now used for public relations rather than lifesaving. The 11-meter (35-foot) boat was built specifically to work in the heavy surf off west Vancouver Island. It did not have radar when it was launched in 1951, so the crew had to feel their way through heavy fogs with pike poles until 1960, when radar was installed. It participated in more than 1,200 rescue incidents during its 40 years of service.

The inshore rescue boat is a rigid-hull inflatable, something of a cross between the well-known Zodiac and a speedboat, a fiberglass V-hull with inflatable tubes attached. The flexible sides make the rescue boats suitable for picking people out of the water and going alongside pitching boats with little fear of damage. Inshore rescue boats have a range of six hours. The coxswain and the two crew members are trained at the Coast Guard School at Bamfield. They spend two weeks on and two weeks off duty.

Five of these vessels are in service and stationed at Victoria, Gabriola Island, Pender Harbour, Port McNeill, and Desolation Sound.

Canadian Coast Guard Inshore Rescue Boat

Length	18 to 24 feet
Beam	N/A
Draft	N/A
Propulsion	Gas; 2 × 70 HP or 2 × 140 HP
Speed	30 to 40 knots
Construction	Fiberglass V-hull with inflatable tubes
Crew	3

SAFETY WORKBOATS

U.S. COAST GUARD SURF BOATS

The most spectacular work performed among all the boats along the coast belongs to the United States and Canadian coast guards's family of rescue boats. They're officially called motor lifeboats, but almost everyone calls them surf boats because that is where they perform the dangerous task of saving lives. These boats come in various lengths and configurations, but the most famous surf boat on the U.S. West Coast is probably the 44-foot version, which carries a crew of four. These boats have saved thousands of lives and prevented property damage that would have amounted to millions of dollars; between 1980 and 1988 they were involved in saving more than 5,000 lives nationwide. The boats have a range of 150 nautical miles and a passenger capacity of 250. Boaters along the Columbia River feel very proprietary toward them because every one of the surf boat coxswains in service was trained at the Cape Disappointment station on the north side of the Columbia River estuary.

The Columbia River entrance, or bar, is two miles wide and runs four miles upriver. This is the most treacherous place for boats along the West Coast. Waves of 10 to 14 feet are normal; 20-foot waves are common. The Coast Guard has hundreds of calls each year to help recreational boaters and commercial fishermen who have overturned, lost their power, or are simply unable to make headway against the seas.

The cadets at the station like to say, "You have to go out, but you don't have to come back." When the call is from a boater in the estuary of a river or in the surf, surf boats always go out. When asked if there are any conditions under which the Coast Guard won't go out, the guard replies simply and directly: not when a human life is in danger. Because their training is so thorough and their equipment so rugged, the Coast Guard performs many successful rescues and doesn't lose many of their crew.

The 44-footers were introduced in 1961, and three decades later, 25 of them are stationed along the Oregon and Washington coasts. Many of them will soon be replaced by a 47-foot aluminum boat. The prototype was built in 1990 and will be tested for three or four years before going into service. It will have improved flotation and self-righting features and will be almost twice as fast, with a top speed of 28 knots.

The other Coast Guard boats often seen along the coastal waterways are the 35-foot fireboat; the 41-foot utility boat used for law enforcement, fishery patrol, and pollution investigation; the 52-foot motor lifeboat, which works offshore; and the 82-foot cutter with a crew of nine that serves essentially the same function as the 41-foot utility boat in law enforcement and fishery patrol.

United States Coast Guard Surf Boat

Length	44 feet
Beam	12 feet
Draft	3 feet
Propulsion	200 HP
Speed	16 knots
Construction	Steel
Crew	4

THE TRIUMPH TRAGEDY

The winter of 1961–62 had more severe storms than any time in memory, and they were especially bad that December. Two brothers, Bert and Stanley Bergman, owned the *Mermaid*, a 40-foot crabber, and they had set several crab pots on the bottom of the Columbia estuary. The pots had been untended for several days while the brothers waited for the weather to improve. Finally they felt they could wait no longer; they went out even though storm-warning flags were up and standing stiff in the gales. Just after they reached their pots, heavy seas broke the rudder on their crabber, and they radioed the Coast Guard for help.

The first boat out was a 44-footer with a crew of three from the Point Adams station on the Oregon side of the Columbia. They crossed the river and went over the bar into the open ocean, found the *Mermaid*, and got a towline on her. The seas were too much for the surf boat, and they couldn't make headway. They radioed for assistance, and a 52-footer named the *Triumph* and a 36-footer went out to help. When the 52-footer arrived, the two smaller boats ran for cover, but the 44-footer capsized before it could find sheltered water. At that time the crew

didn't have survival suits, nor were they tethered to their vessels, so all three crew members went into the sea. The crew on the 36-footer saw them go over and were able to retrieve them. The boat, however, was lost.

In the meantime, the struggle between the *Triumph* and the sea continued, and the sea was winning. Darkness came, and with it, winds that held steady at 75 knots and gusts that went off the gauges. The 52-footer's radio antennas snapped off, and men back at the stations hovered around their radios, afraid of what the silence meant.

The 213-foot cutter *Yacona* was sent out from its base several miles away in Astoria, Oregon, and the skipper told his crew that they must assume that "all boats are down and the men in the water."

The men aboard the *Yacona* took a terrible beating as they steamed out into the night. When the spray hit them, it felt like sand in a desert storm, and walls of water crashed over the bridge 42 feet above the waterline. Fire extinguishers were ripped from their mounts and thrashed wildly around the ship. Fire hoses snapped and whipped like snakes.

Suddenly, in the midst of this, the *Yacona* crew saw the

Mermaid and the *Triumph*. Something had happened to the towline, and the men on the cutter could see four of the five *Triumph* crew members on deck as the coxswain fought to turn the boat around and put another towline on the *Mermaid*. They could also see one of the Bergman brothers clinging to the bow, waiting to catch the line.

Then one of the men on the cutter spotted what he thought was a light in the water, and since their first responsibility was to a person in the water, the *Yacona* turned to search for him. Nobody was there.

Just after the *Yacona* turned, the *Triumph* capsized, and a nearby 36-footer rushed over. Before it got there, the *Mermaid* capsized, too. The *Yacona* and the smaller boats hovered around the area using searchlights and flares, but found no survivors. Later they discovered that only one man had survived the multiple sinkings. Gordon Higgins of the *Triumph* was below, checking the engines, when it went over. The boat eventually righted itself, and Higgins held on until it ran aground near the North Head lighthouse. He was rescued sometime after daybreak by the beach patrol sent out to search for survivors and bodies.

The 36-footer that had made the last attempt to save the *Mermaid* was badly damaged, and the coxswain knew he'd never make it across the bar and back to base. His nearest haven was the lightship *Columbia*, anchored at its fixed location off the river's mouth. He made a dash for the ship and miraculously was able to find it and pull alongside. His damaged boat sank only minutes after the crew climbed aboard the pitching ship.

The night's toll was seven men and four boats. Only one body was discovered, that of the *Triumph*'s coxswain. The only other evidence found from the disaster was a door from the *Triumph* that washed up on the beach.

The tragedy most likely wouldn't happen with today's improved boats and the use of helicopters. Today's 30- and 44-footers are built with heavy keels, which make them both self-righting and self-bailing. Boaters who have experienced an overturn say that the 18 to 20 seconds it takes the boat to right itself is an eternity and that it is extremely noisy underwater. The crew wear survival suits and strap themselves to the boat with harnesses when they go into heavy surf.

SAFETY WORKBOATS

BUOY TENDERS

While the Coast Guard's fleet of small craft gets a lot of attention for saving lives and boats along the coastline, the service has other vessels that perform equally important but less dramatic duties. Buoy tenders, for example, perform the critical job of maintaining navigational aids, although the public seldom hears of them.

Tenders service the navigational buoys that mark the shipping channels on inland waters. Crews are also sent ashore in small boats to take care of shore-based navigational aids. This can entail everything from fixing a foghorn to cutting branches so that a neon mark on the beach can be seen by boaters.

Buoys have gone through several generations, from oil lamps to acetylene to electric batteries to the present system of solar-powered lights, radio beacons, and horns. The tenders are equipped to clean, repair, and replace all parts of the various types of buoys after they are hoisted onto the tender's deck with a boom. On the 180-foot tender shown here, the boom capacity is 20 tons.

The U.S. Coast Guard employs tenders on all coasts and in the Great Lakes, and at least ten 180-foot tenders are stationed along the West Coast in the

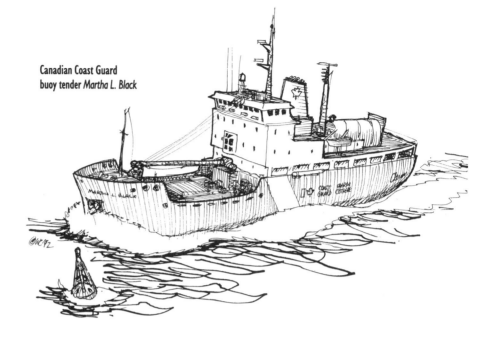

Canadian Coast Guard
buoy tender *Martha L. Black*

following ports: San Pedro and San Francisco, California; Astoria, Oregon; Seattle, Washington; and Ketchikan and Kodiak, Alaska. These vessels are all of similar design, and all were built in 1943 and 1944 by two companies in Duluth, Minnesota — the Zenith Dredge Company and Marine Iron & Shipbuilding Corporation — at a cost of between $860,000 and $950,000 apiece. In addition to servicing buoys and aids, Coast Guard tenders assist in ice breaking and search-and-rescue operations.

Buoy Tender

Length	180 feet
Beam	37 feet
Draft	13 feet
Propulsion	Diesel-electric; 1,200 HP
Speed	13.5 knots
Construction	Steel
Crew	3 officers, 2 warrants, 42 sailors

LARGE WORKBOATS

DREDGES

A century ago the Northern Pacific railroad reached Portland, Oregon, establishing it as a more important seaport than Astoria, even though it was 105 miles from the mouth of the Columbia River. The Oregon legislature created the Port of Portland and began funneling money into it to attract shipping business. In 1898, the port was given funds for the purchase of a dredge to keep the shipping channel clear to the sea. At that time the Columbia's average depth was 12 feet, but shifting sandbars and shoals were everywhere beneath the murky water, making navigation hazardous.

The Port of Portland employed the *Portland*, a wood-burning, steam-powered dredge. It was joined in 1902 by the *Columbia I*, almost three times as powerful. A third dredge, the *Willamette I*, was launched in 1912. The *Tualatin* went to work in 1916, the *Columbia II* in 1921, and the *Clackamas* in 1925.

Today the *Oregon*, which was launched in 1965, is the only dredge owned by the Port of Portland. It looks something like those magnificent paddlewheel steamboats of the last century, with its boxy construction, two decks, and tall superstructure rising to a height of 11½ feet. It can be found along the Columbia, with its floating pipeline running to shore, as its powerful pump sucks up mud and silt from the bottom of the river and pumps it ashore to sites selected to receive the dredge spoils, or depots where the spoils will be trucked away. The *Oregon* can dredge up to 85 feet deep, pumping the spoils up to 8,000 feet at a capacity of 35,000 cubic yards per 24 hours. Unlike the other dredges discussed here, the *Oregon* is not self-propelled and requires a considerable attendant plant, including a 65-foot towboat, a 55-foot power barge, a 35-foot crew boat (see "Small Workboats: Crew Boats") launch, five anchor barges, over 18,000 feet of pipeline, a water barge, and a fuel barge.

The dredge's biggest job came in May 1980, when Mount St. Helens erupted and dumped a load of ash, sand, and debris of biblical proportions into the Toutle River, which feeds into the Cowlitz River, a tributary of the Columbia that enters at Kelso–Longview, Washington. The flood of volcanic material raced down the mountain at 30 miles per hour and into the rivers, forming a shoal of sand and debris all the way across the Columbia's navigation channel. For a space of 7 miles, the remaining channel was only about 15 feet deep; the day before the eruption, it had been 40 feet deep. Ships were stranded on either side of this dam; those in Kalama, Washington, and Portland could not leave, and those downstream couldn't move upriver.

The dredge *Oregon* and the U.S. Army Corps of Engineers's three hopper dredges went to work, and in five days they had cleared a channel wide and deep enough for small ships to pass. It took them six weeks to return the channel to its normal 40-foot depth and 600-foot width.

One benefit of river dredging is the new land created by the dredge spoils. All along the river between Portland and Astoria are new islands, beaches, and industrial sites. These include Rivergate Industrial District, Swan Island Industrial Park, Port of Portland terminals, Portland International Airport, and similar areas near Vancouver, Kalama, Longview (all in Washington), and Astoria.

Dredge *Oregon*

Length	Hull: 180 feet; with ladder, spuds: 296 feet
Beam	52 feet
Power	Diesel; 4,985 HP
Speed	N/A
Construction	Steel
Crew	39, plus galley crew when needed

LARGE WORKBOATS

HOPPER DREDGES

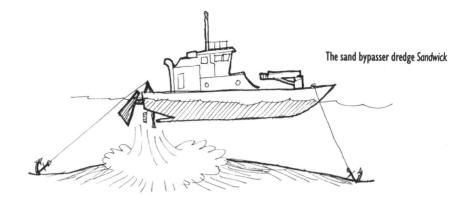

The sand bypasser dredge *Sandwick*

The U.S. Army Corps of Engineers has three hopper dredges assigned to the Portland district, which covers all of Oregon's harbors along the Pacific coast and up the Columbia River to The Dalles. Unlike the Port of Portland's dredge, *Oregon*, which must be moved by a towboat, these dredges are small ships outfitted with dredging equipment. Two of them have large hoppers to store the dredge spoils until they can be dumped in deep water or ashore.

The smallest, the 74-foot *Sandwick*, is more accurately called a sand bypasser rather than a dredge because it works something like a spawning fish; it agitates the river bottom with its propeller to clear a shoal to a depth of 21 feet. The rectangular boat is shaped like a military landing craft, and on the square stern is a steel plate called a thrust plate that can be lowered into the water just behind the propeller. The prop wash hits this plate and is forced downward. The scouring action causes the sediment on the river bottom to rise in the water and be washed away by the current.

With a shallow draft of just under 6 feet, the *Sandwick* can work most river bars along the coast and keep channels open at small fishing ports. The *Sandwick* has a cruising range of 300 nautical miles. It sometimes enters a channel ahead of its larger sister dredges, the *Yaquina* and the *Essayons*, in order to open the channel for them.

Often when the *Sandwick* is caught in a strong current, the crew throws out four anchors, one at each corner, to maintain the dredge's position. These weigh 1,500 pounds each and are controlled by winches. This anchoring ability is especially useful when the boat is being used for chores in addition to dredging. For example, the *Sandwick* is used as a stable platform for taking core samples used in dredging studies and for engineering the construction of locks and bridges.

Hopper Dredge *Sandwick*

Length	74 feet
Beam	21 feet 10 inches
Draft	5 feet 8 inches
Propulsion	Diesel; 2 × 520 HP
Speed	12 knots
Construction	Steel
Crew	3

The dredge *Yaquina*, operated by the Portland District U.S. Army Corps of Engineers

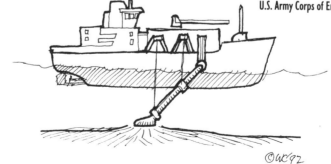

©WC92

Next largest of these three Army Corps of Engineers hopper dredges is the 200-foot *Yaquina*. With a 58-foot beam and a draft of only 8 feet, it was acquired in 1981 to work in the smaller rivers and harbors along the Washington, Oregon, and California coastlines. It is the most automated of the dredges, with an untended engine room. In addition, much of its dredging operation is accomplished with a semiautomatic system and instrumentation that allows it to operate 24 hours a day.

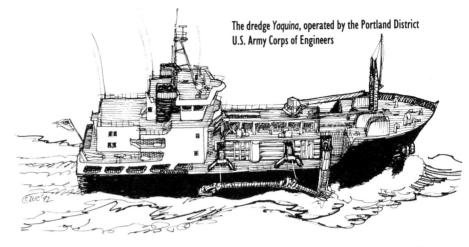

The dredge *Yaquina*, operated by the Portland District U.S. Army Corps of Engineers

Hopper Dredge *Yaquina*

Length	200 feet
Beam	58 feet
Draft	8 feet
Propulsion	Diesel; 2 × 1,125 HP
Speed	11 knots
Construction	Steel
Crew	29

The *Yaquina* accomplishes the same job as the stationary dredge *Oregon* but is totally self-contained. It has dragarms that hang from each side of the vessel with a draghead at the tip. These are slowly pulled over a shallow area, and pumps create suction in the dragarm that pulls the silt and sand into the hopper bins. The *Yaquina* can dredge to a 45- to 55-foot depth. When the hopper is filled to its 825-cubic-yard capacity, the dredge runs to the disposal area and dumps the spoils from large hopper doors in the bottom of the vessel.

The dredge normally works continuously for 12 days and then ties up for two days for fuel, water, supplies, and maintenance. The 29-member crew works 10 days on and 4 days off.

The *Essayons* is the largest of the hopper dredge fleet of three and was delivered in 1981. It clears the entrance bars and harbors, particularly of the larger rivers in the three West Coast states in addition to Alaska and Hawaii. Like the *Yaquina*, it is highly automated, with an unattended engine room and semiautomatic dragarm handling system that enables it to work around the clock. The crew of 25 works one week on and one week off.

The *Essayons* has a hopper capacity of 6,000 cubic yards. In addition to the hopper doors at the bottom of the vessel, the *Essayons* can also pump out its load.

Hopper Dredge *Essayons*

Length	350 feet
Beam	68 feet
Draft	22 feet
Propulsion	Diesel; 2 × 3,600 HP
Construction	Steel
Speed	13.8 knots
Crew	25

Day's work consists, at least, of the dead reckoning from noon to noon,
morning and afternoon time sights for longitude, and a meridian altitude for latitude.
Gershom Bradford, *The Mariner's Dictionary*

SUPPLY VESSELS

From the rear, the supply boat *Rig Engineer* looks like a cross between a barge and a tug, which is about what it is, with its keel, sharp bow, and generous bargelike deck. The vessel's job is to run supplies, drilling water, and people to the offshore oil platforms in Alaska's Cook Inlet. Most recently it has been used as a tug supply boat, working mainly in the Chukchi Sea.

The *Rig Engineer* can carry 19 passengers in comfortable quarters, 146,000 gallons of potable water, and 110,000 gallons of fuel.

This supply boat is as sturdy as a rock, with an ice-strengthened hull and 3,625 square feet of deck space. It also has a bow thruster — a water-jet pump that gives it greater control while docking and coming alongside platforms or other vessels. A crew of eight operates the *Rig Engineer*, with half of the crew on duty at a time.

Supply Vessel *Rig Engineer*

Length	165 feet
Beam	36 feet
Draft	15 feet
Propulsion	Diesel; 2 × 2,250 HP
Speed	12 knots
Construction	Steel
Crew	8

LARGE WORKBOATS

SNAGBOATS

The U.S. Army Corps of Engineers's snagboat, *Puget*, has a simple design to reflect its simple function: to pick up debris—mostly stray logs, waterlogged pilings, and tree stumps—that impedes or endangers small craft and ships in rivers and in Puget Sound. This job description calls for a self-propelled barge with a pilothouse and crane.

The *Puget* occasionally works as a pile driver, and it has a clamshell dredging bucket for clearing clogged channels. It is also used for exploratory drilling for foundations.

The *Puget* is the fourth snagboat assigned to Puget Sound and its tributary rivers. The first was a raft built in 1880, with a Congressional appropriation of $2,500, to clear an enormous logjam that was blocking the Skagit River. The raft was built upriver and fitted with a derrick and hand-operated capstan. Then it was floated down to the logjam. The crew controlled the raft's speed and direction with steering oars and by dragging a heavy log chain from the stern. When the crew wanted to stop, they heaved a heavy anchor over the side and hoped for the best. In spite of its primitive technology, the raft was successful.

In 1885 Congress appropriated $20,000 for a proper snagboat, and the steam-powered paddle wheeler *Skagit* was built. It had a stationary crane on the bow and a long foredeck for storing snags and other debris. The *Skagit* ran until 1914, when it was replaced by another paddle wheeler, the *Swinomish*. This in turn was replaced by the steam-powered paddle wheeler *Preston*, which served 52 years, until the *Puget* took over in 1981. The old *Preston* was retired and now is the centerpiece of a nautical museum in Anacortes, Washington.

The *Puget* was built in 1944 by the Navy as a yard derrick. It was acquired by the Corps of Engineers in 1968 and remodeled to its present configuration, including a 39-foot mast. The *Puget* has a crane capacity of 20 tons and a crane boom length of 70 feet. It works on the sheltered waters of Puget Sound and Lake Washington, from Olympia to the Canadian border.

The crew picks up an average of 14 tons of debris a day, more than 2,600 tons per year. Some of the material, particularly creosote-treated pilings, is hauled to approved landfills. Some timber is taken to mills and turned into wood chips.

The *Puget* responds to special calls to remove debris, but its normal schedule is a monthly patrol from Bellingham to Olympia. Although the vessel has bunks aboard, it is not designed for overnight use, so when it is away from the Seattle area, the crew sleeps ashore. When not in use, the *Puget* is moored at the Hiram Chittenden Locks in Seattle. A smaller vessel, the *Walton*, substitutes for the *Puget* when it is in dry dock.

The *Puget* has two virtually identical sister ships in San Francisco Bay, the *Coyote* and the *Raccoon*.

Snagboat *Puget*

Length	104 feet
Beam	30 feet
Draft	4 feet unloaded
Propulsion	Diesel; 2 × 335 HP
Speed	6 knots
Construction	Steel
Crew	4 to 5

PILE DRIVERS

Although pile drivers are not boats because they are not self-propelled, the definition of workboats can be stretched a bit to include them because pile drivers are certainly working crafts, even if they must be moved from place to place by a tug. They are used wherever construction is under way along the waterfront, where repairs are needed to waterfront buildings, bridges, piers, and especially ferry docks, which take a terrible beating.

A pile driver drives pilings — long telephone pole–like logs that have been pressure-treated with creosote so that they won't be consumed by the ever-present teredoes in the water — into the floor of the sea. The pilings are set into place and then literally hammered. Most newer pile drivers are operated by air pressure, which lifts and then drives the hammer down. The hammer is suspended in a guide, or "gin." Older pile drivers are operated by steam- or diesel-powered engines that turn a drum that winds up the cable to lift the hammer; then it is released.

A typical pile driver will have a crew of five or six: the operator, the foreman, and three or four pile bucks to handle the rigging, chain saws, and power tools and perform other construction and repair chores.

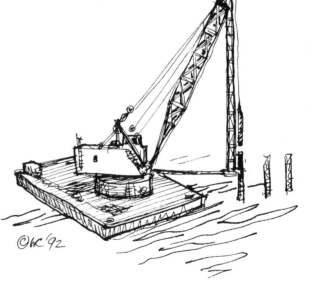

Auto carriers carry 2,000 to 4,000 new automobiles from Japan and Korea to the West Coast, making them floating parking garages. When the ships dock, the cars are driven off. On their return trips, auto carriers are sometimes filled with other American products. The ships are up to 600 feet long, 100 feet wide, and at least 150 feet tall. They are often called "ro-ro" ships because their cargo rolls on and rolls off.

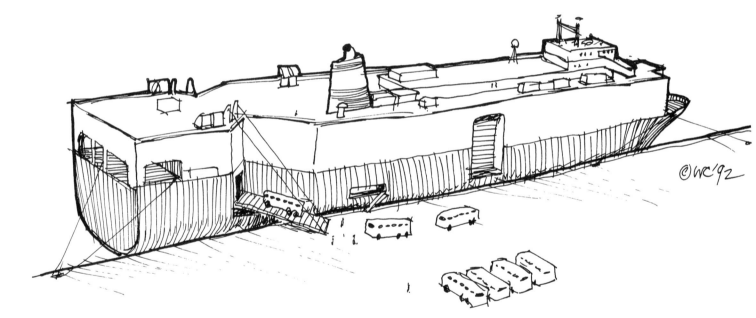

Bulk carriers carry any dry cargo that is shipped in bulk: grain, ore, salt, and coal, to name a few. Bulkers frequently have no cargo gear or crane. They are dependent on shore facilities to load and discharge their cargoes. The ships anchored off Magnolia Bluff in Seattle's Elliott Bay and off English Bay outside of Vancouver, B.C. are probably bulkers waiting for their turn at the grain elevators.

Breakbulk carriers carry a wide variety of dry cargoes that are stowed by hand or by means of forklifts. They have their own cranes for moving the cargo, which may be anything from containers to boxes of apples, crude rubber, or bags of seed wheat. Boxed, bagged, or bundled cargoes are common. The ships average about 500 feet long.

Oil tankers (shown here) are liquid bulkers. They come in two distinct types. The crude carrier is designed for shipping a single grade of crude oil from Valdez, the Persian Gulf, or Indonesia to refineries in north Puget Sound, San Francisco Bay, or the greater port of Los Angeles. Product carriers, on the other hand, deliver refined petroleum — gasolines, jet fuel, stove oil, etc. — from refineries to distribution centers from which it is trucked or barged until it finally finds its way to your local gas station.

The crude carriers are normally very large ships. The product carrier is a smaller, more versatile vessel capable of carrying different grades of oil or products in totally segregated systems.

106

Container ships carry containers that can be transferred to trains or trucks without being opened. Containers are usually 20 feet or 40 feet long, 8 feet wide, and 8½ to 9½ feet high. These boxes, when married to a chassis, become a highway semitrailer. Container ships come in all sizes. Some are over 700 feet long. Cruising at 24 knots, these ships can travel from Puget Sound to Anchorage in 72 hours.

The smaller ships may be able to load and unload their containers at smaller ports with shipboard mounted cranes.

Most large container vessels depend on large gantry cranes (shown below), now found in every major world port.

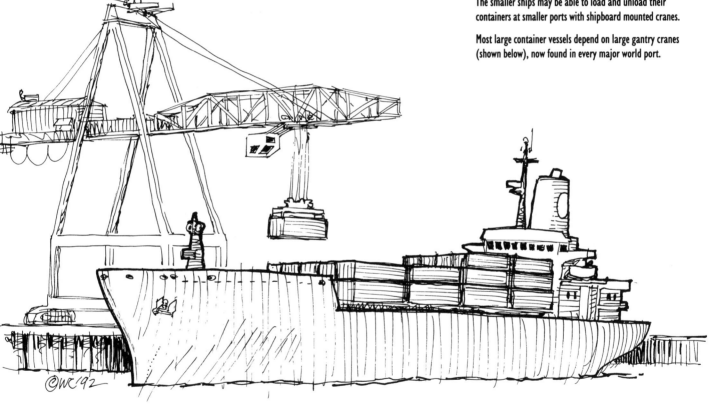

Cruise ships offer summer service to southeastern and south central Alaska destinations. They are large, modern ships offering first-class accommodations to the vacation traveler. In the winter, many of these same ships operate from Florida to ports in the Caribbean. Because the fleet of Alaska cruise ships is under foreign registry, the ships are prohibited by U.S. laws from carrying passengers between two U.S. ports. This is the reason Vancouver, B.C. has become the principal embarkation point for many of the cruise ships headed north to Alaska.

ALPHABET FLAGS

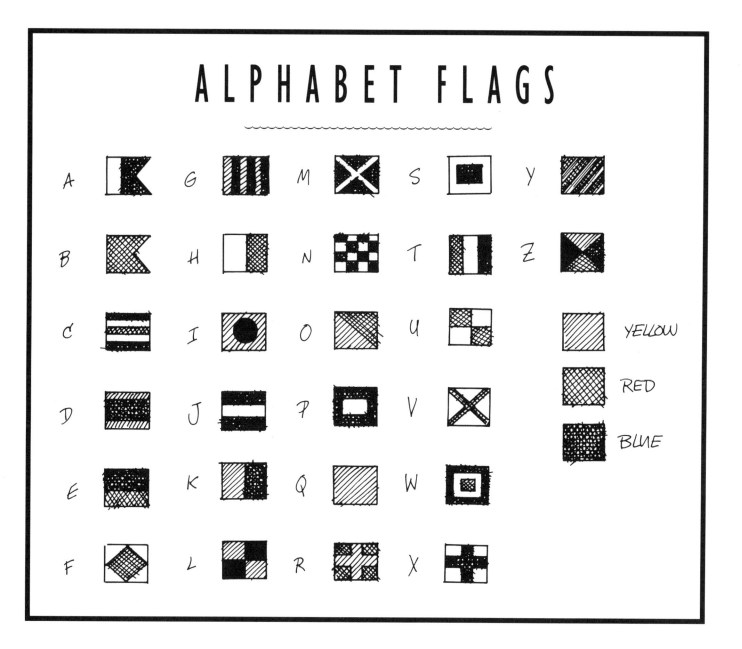

GLOSSARY

Aft:
Toward or at the stern of a vessel.

Amidships:
Midway between the bow and the stern as well as midway between port and starboard.

Antiroll tank:
A system used on boats and ships that moves fuel or ballast water back and forth between tanks to stabilize the vessel in heavy weather.

Bait cutter:
Machine used to cut bait fish into chunks of the proper size and shape for baiting hooks.

Baiter:
See *Hook baiter*.

Ballast:
Weight, usually seawater, carried in a vessel to provide stability or ensure proper trim.

Bar:
The place in an estuary where the river's current meets the ocean waves, often forming a shoal of sand or gravel.

Barge:
A flat-bottomed vessel, usually unpowered, that is towed or pushed by tugboats.

Beam:
The width of a vessel at the widest point.

Block:
A pulley. See also *Power block*.

Boom:
A spar, usually attached to a mast, used for lifting cargo and equipment; also, a long spar extending the length of the foot of a sail.

Boom sticks:
Logs that are chained together to form a log boom.

Boomboat:
Another name for *pond boat*.

Booming beaver:
Another name for *pond boat*.

Bow:
The front section of a vessel.

Bow thruster:
A propeller mounted transversely in the forefoot of a vessel. Used during docking maneuvers in lieu of a tug.

Bowpicker:
A type of *gill-netter* that retrieves the net over the bow.

Bridge:
A raised platform on a vessel, where the steering wheel, navigational equipment, and propulsion controls are located.

Buoy:
A floating marker or navigational device that is anchored in one spot.

Buoy tender:
A vessel dedicated to the upkeep and repair of buoys.

Capstan:
A rotating cylinder used for hauling in rope or line or for hoisting heavy loads.

Catamaran:
A vessel with twin hulls.

Clipper:
A fast sailing ship; traditionally, one with a long, slender hull, tall masts, and a large sail area.

Construction:
In this book's specification tables, refers to materials the vessel is made of.

Coxswain:
A crew member who is in charge of the crew and who, in a small boat, acts as helmsman.

Crab pot:
A trap for crabs.

Crabber:
A fishing boat outfitted for dropping crab pots overboard and retrieving them.

Crew:
In this book's specification tables, refers to the number of individuals needed to operate each boat.

Crew boat:
A small boat designed to transport crews or individuals; a taxi boat.

Crow's nest:
The place or position on a mast where a crew member can stand and watch for fish or other vessels.

Cruising range:
The distance a vessel can travel without refueling.

Current:
A flow of water in a definite direction.

Cutter:
A small, armed vessel in government service.

Cycloidal propeller:
A propeller whose position, or pitch, in relation to the hull can be adjusted to drive the ship in the desired direction. A vessel with a cycloidal propeller is rudderless, because the propeller provides steerage as well as power. See also *Fixed-pitch propeller*.

Deadweight tonnage:
The total weight a vessel can load, including fuel, cargo, stores, crew, and passengers.

Deck:
The platform that extends from one side of a boat's hull to the other, forming the main horizontal surface area of the vessel and the floors of the *deckhouses*.

Deckhouse:
An enclosed structure, such as a cabin or other compartment, built on the deck of a ship.

Dogs:
A nickname for the steel teeth on the front of small tugs, used for shunting logs. Also, a means of securing a door or hatch aboard a ship.

Door:
A device attached to the mouth of a trawl net to keep the net open.

Dory:
A flat-bottomed rowing boat with pointed bow, raked or V-shaped stern, and high, flaring sides.

Double-ended:
Type of vessel in which the stern is shaped similar to the bow, such as a canoe.

Draft:
The vertical distance from the keel to the waterline.

Dredge:
A vessel used to dig or deepen channels.

Dredge spoils:
Material picked up from the river or sea bottom by dredges and pumped or deposited ashore or in deep water.

Dry dock:
A structure that supports a vessel out of water, used for construction or repair of the vessel.

Factory processor:
A large vessel on which fish are cleaned and frozen or processed while still fresh. Some factory processors can both catch and process fish; others buy the catch from other fishing boats.

Fathom:
A measure of depth equal to six feet.

Ferry:
A passenger boat, often with vehicle-carrying capability; sometimes open- and/or double-ended.

Filterbelt:
The name for a patented conveyor belt system that picks up spilled oil from water.

Fireboat:
A boat designed to fight fires.

Fixed-pitch propeller:
A propeller with fixed blades usually cast as a single piece. See also *Cycloidal propeller*.

Flasher:
The brightly colored piece of metal on a fishing line, designed to attract the attention of fish. The flasher precedes the bait.

Forward:
Toward the bow (front) of a vessel.

Freeboard:
The distance from the water's surface to the main deck, properly measured at the center of the vessel.

Gaff:
A hand-held sharp hook for bringing fish aboard.

Gantry:
A frame built across the width of a vessel from which blocks or other gear is suspended. A gantry crane is a crane on which the load is suspended from a traveling trolley.

Gill net:
Fishing net designed to snare fish by their gills as they swim into it. The net is suspended in the water with buoyed and weighted edges, so it acts like a fence.

Gill-netter:
A boat used for fishing with gill nets.

Guidon:
A pole protruding ahead of the pilothouse of a ferry, used for relative steering by sight.

Gurdy:
A power-operated winch for hauling line aboard long-liners and trollers.

Halyard:
Rope, or line, and tackles, usually attached to the mast and used for hoisting and lowering items such as equipment or sails.

Header:
The boom stick (log) that goes across the rear end of a log boom.

Helmsman:
The person responsible for steering a vessel.

Hook baiter:
A device that automatically attaches bait to hooks.

Hopper dredge:
A bargelike vessel outfitted with dredging equipment; spoils are stored in the hoppers.

Hovercraft:
A vessel that operates on a cushion of air created by powerful fans.

Hull:
The main body or frame of a vessel, separate from masts, rigging, decking, and so forth.

Hydraulic:
Operated by the pressure created when a liquid is forced through an aperture or tube.

Inboard:
Within the perimeter of the hull, as in an inboard engine. See also *Outboard*.

Inboard-outboard:
A permanently mounted inboard engine connected through the transom to an outdrive or Z-drive.

Keel:
The lowest continuous section of vessel; extends from or along the bottom of the hull.

Kicker boat:
An aluminum skiff.

Knot:
A measure of speed that is equal to one nautical mile (6,080 feet) per hour or 1.15 statute miles per hour.

Leader:
The section of high-strength line, usually made of steel, that attaches the hook to the fishing line.

Length:
In this book's specification tables, refers to *length overall*.

Length on waterline (LW):
The length of a vessel's hull as measured at the waterline.

Length overall (LOA):
The greatest overall length of a vessel's hull, measured from bow to stern.

Lightship:
A ship that acts as a navigational aid. A lightship has brilliant lights and is moored or anchored near a navigational hazard. Most lightships have been replaced by large buoys.

Line of demarcation:
The line between two points where the rules of international and inland waters meet.

Line pull:
Measurement of the pulling power of a vessel, such as a tug.

Lock:
An enclosed area of water with gates at both ends. Water can be let in or out, to raise or lower vessels from one level to the next through a canal or around a dam.

Lockage:
The maximum-size load that can be taken through a navigational lock.

Log boom:
See *Log raft*.

Log bronc:
Another name for *pond boat*.

Log raft:
Logs bundled together to be transported by water.

Longline:
A long fishing line with a series of hooks attached to it.

Long-liner:
A fishing boat that strings out longlines.

Lure:
The bait, artificial or real, for catching fish.

Mast:
A vertical spar on a vessel, used for carrying sails, for hauling aboard cargo or equipment, or for carrying navigational lights or signals.

Masthead:
The top of a mast.

Monitor:
A fire-fighting nozzle on a stationary mount.

Monohull:
A single-hulled vessel.

Net drum:
Powered (usually hydraulically) drum used to pull nets in.

Net reel:
See *Net drum*.

Oil spill recovery vessel:
A vessel designed to clean up oil spills with skimmers or other devices.

Outboard:
Outside the perimeter of a vessel, as in an outboard engine.

Outrigger:
A framework supporting a float for stability or a similar device.

Pike pole:
A pole with a sharp point and hook, used by workers in log ponds.

Pilothouse:
The deckhouse from which the helmsman steers the vessel; houses the steering wheel, compass, and navigational equipment.

Pitch:
The position or angle of the propeller in relation to the hull.

Pond boat:
A small boat used to move logs in a storage pond. Also called *boomboat* or *booming beaver*.

Port:
The left side of a vessel, facing the bow.

Power block:
A pulley that is powered, usually hydraulically; often used to haul a purse seine.

Power takeoff:
A device attached to an engine that supplies power to a stationary mechanism such as a pump.

Propulsion:
That which propels, or moves, the vessel through the water; usually described as the type and number of engines and shafts with propellers.

Psi:
Pounds per square inch.

Purse seine:
A net with lines that pull together the bottom, similar to a string purse, thus encircling the fish. A purse seiner is a fishing boat that uses purse seines.

Pushboat:
A boat that pushes rather than tows its load.

Radar:
An electronic device that uses ultrahigh-frequency radio waves to locate and track objects, such as the shoreline, buoys, or other vessels.

Range:
See *Cruising range*.

Reef net:
The nets strung between two stationary floats.

Rigging:
All the lines, ropes, cables, and hardware that support the masts and spars of a vessel and that are used to raise and lower sails.

Riverboat:
Another name for a *towboat* or *pushboat*.

Rudder:
The broad, flat attachment at a vessel's stern that steers the vessel.

Salvage tug:
A large, versatile tug used to raise sunken vessels, perform underwater repairs, and carry out other emergency procedures.

Scow:
A flat-bottomed, rectangular boat.

Screw:
Another word for a vessel's propeller. Single screw means there is one propeller, twin screws means there are two.

Seiner:
A fishing boat that uses a purse seine as a net.

Self-righting:
A boat designed to right itself when it turns over.

Skeg:
The stern or aft section of the keel. (Also the fin at the rear bottom of a surfboard.)

Skiff:
A small, light rowboat.

Skimmer:
A boat that picks up oil that has been spilled onto water.

Snag association:
A portion of the Columbia River kept free of snags and debris by fishermen who constantly maintain the area.

Snagboat:
A boat designed to pick up and dispose of logs and other debris found in inland waters.

Spar:
Any of the rounded wood, aluminum, or metal pieces used to support a ship's rigging, such as a mast, boom, or yard.

Speed:
In this book, speed is given in *knots* and usually reflects the design speed of the given vessel.

Starboard:
The right side of a vessel, facing the bow.

Stern:
The rear section of a vessel.

Superseiner:
The newest class of tuna clippers.

Supply vessel:
A large workboat that runs supplies, water, and people to other vessels, isolated villages, and offshore oil platforms.

Surf boat:
The U.S. Coast Guard boats designed for rescues in heavy seas close to shore.

Survival suit:
An insulated suit that a sailor wears when in the ocean.

Swifters:
Steel cables used to tie log booms together.

Tender:
A vessel used to attend to other vessels or to navigational aids. A tender may supply provisions, provide communication between a larger ship and the shore, or attend to maintenance and upkeep of buoys.

Teredo:
A worm that lives in salt water and attacks wood that hasn't been treated by creosote or other preservatives.

Towboat:
A powerful boat that pushes, rather than pulls, other vessels or barges.

Tractor tug:
A tug with either a cycloidal propeller or Z-drive.

Transom:
The vertical, flat portion of a boat's stern.

Trawl nets:
A cone-shaped net towed behind the fishing boat at a depth controlled by weights. Devices called *doors* keep the mouth of the net open.

Trawler:
A fishing boat that uses trawl nets.

Troller:
A boat that fishes by trailing hooked lines.

Trotline:
A line from which several baited hooks dangle while it is left in position several hours. Used in long-lining.

Tugboat:
A powerful boat used for pushing or pulling through the water other vessels, barges, or cargo such as log rafts.

Tuna clipper:
A large, swift fishing boat built especially for the tuna industry.

Tuna seiner:
Another name for *tuna clipper*.

Waterline:
The level of the water on the outside of the hull. The load waterline is marked on a vessel and indicates the depth to which a vessel can be safely loaded.

Wheelhouse:
See *Pilothouse*.

Winch:
A rotating cylinder used for spooling rope or line.

Yard derrick:
A crane mounted on a barge for use in a shipyard.

Z-drive:
A combined steering and propulsion system using one or more propellers that can be turned in any direction.

Zodiac:
A trademarked word to describe an inflatable boat.

ACKNOWLEDGMENTS

When you begin researching a subject with an empty notebook, you must emulate Blanche DuBois and rely on the kindness of strangers. Most of the strangers I met while writing this book were helpful and patient. Nobody treated my questions as though they were dumb, and several individuals tolerated my repeated phone calls for information I should have asked for the first time I called.

I have tried to make note of all the people who helped me, and if I lost a scrap of paper with a name on it before it could be committed to this manuscript, I apologize. Most were generous with their time and knowledge, and if errors appear, the fault is mine.

I wish to thank Theresa Morrow, editor, *Marine Digest*; Robert Carpenter, editor, *WorkBoat*; Rob Morris, editor, and Alan Haig-Brown, vice president, *West Coast Mariner* magazine (Haig-Brown, the author of several popular books about boats, had planned to write a book identical to this one and was still generous with information); Bill Munson, president, Munson Manufacturing Company; Dave Ritchie, port engineer, Middle Rock, Inc.; Dick Montgomery, Judy Johnson, and Myrla Maness, Port of Portland; Bill Stevens, manager, and Richard Cole, attorney, Port of Edmonds, Washington; Gary Hansen, Hansen Boat Company; D.W. Lerch, Garth Wilcox, Hal Cook, and J. Lewis VanDeMark, MARCO, Seattle; the public information staff, Port of Tacoma; Charles Nash, San Juan Island; Skip Hart, Tidewater Barge Lines, Portland.

Rick Knight, Samson Tug and Barge; Chuck Curnutt, Foss tugboat skipper on the Snohomish River delta; Mike Skalley, Mike Wilcox, and Donald G. Hogue, Foss Launch & Tug Company, Seattle; Leonard McCann, curator, Vancouver Maritime Museum; Steve Rybeck, public information officer, Canadian Coast Guard, Vancouver, B.C.; David Clegg, Ministry of Public Works, Vancouver, B.C.; U.S. Coast Guard public affairs staff, Seattle; Darnell C. Baldinelli, marine inspector, U.S. Coast Guard; the staff of the Coast Guard Museum, Seattle; Dawn Edwards, U.S. Army Corps of Engineers, Portland; Bill Van Black, wooden boat owner, Seattle; David and Hilda Cullen, who introduced me to Van Black; Rick Hallanger, skipper, and Skip Kimball, deckhand, on Dunlap Towing's *Port Susan*; Steven Canright, curator, National Maritime Museum, San Francisco; Dave Peden, editor, *Oregon Coast* magazine, Newport, Oregon; Erin P. Caldwell, public information officer, British Columbia Ferry Corporation, Vancouver, B.C.; Pat Cook, Department of Fisheries Library, Seattle; Stan Westover, Port of San Diego; Patricia Graesser, public information officer, U.S. Army Corps of Engineers, Seattle; Tina-Marie Pinney, assistant to the president, Campbell Shipyard, San Diego; Jeffrey Serage, boatwright and good traveling companion, Seattle; Eugene Kirsten, son of the cycloidal propeller inventor and owner of Kirsten Pipe Company, Seattle; Cassie Satterfield Adkins, Scott Satterfield, and Sarah Satterfield, survivors of the Alaska fisheries, Seattle; John Mc-Glone, Sea Scout veteran and recently licensed master, Seattle; Dr. Dayton Lee Alverson, Seattle; Oscar Lind, Robert Hale & Company, Bellevue, Washington; Susan Harris, public information officer, Washington State Ferries; Jerry Mecham, port captain, and David Black, assistant port captain, Washington State Ferries; Elmar Baxter, Huntington Beach, California; Knute Jensen, San Francisco Bar Pilots Association; John Bowles, Harken Towing Company Ltd., Port Coquitlan, B.C.; E. A. Robinson, Golden Gate Ferries; Jeff Sidebotham, Seaborn Pile Driving Company; Dick Simpson and Al Anderson, Crowley Marine Corporation; the staffs of the Middle Rock, Puget Sound, Long Beach, San Francisco, San Diego, and Vancouver, B.C., coastal pilots' associations; Carolyn Bosco, Jim Green, and Benny Cope of San Diego Harbor Excursions. Hobe Kytr, educator for the Columbia River Maritime Museum in Astoria, Oregon, generously shared his knowledge of gill-netters gained from an oral history project he conducted.

The illustrator acknowledges the special assistance of Don Wilson, Port of Seattle staff photographer, and Marc Jones, MARCO; the technical guidance of Robert J. Browning's *Fisheries of the North Pacific*; the confidence of the author, Archie Satterfield; the kind intelligence of the editor, Anne Depue; the support of the publisher, Chad Haight; and the matchmaking assistance of one Alex Edelstein.

Thanks also to *Pacific Fishing* and *Pacific Maritime* magazines and to the General Construction Company for the loan of photographs.

Additional Sources

Books

Bannerman, Gary and Patricia. *The Ships of British Columbia*. Surrey, B.C.: Hancock House, 1985.

Blair, Carvel Hall, and Willits Dyer Ansel. *A Guide to Fishing Boats and Their Gear*. Cambridge, Md.: Cornell Maritime Press, 1968.

Browning, Robert J. *Fisheries of the North Pacific*. Anchorage: Alaska Northwest Publishing Company, 1974.

Delbridge, Joyce. *Ferry Tales from Puget Sound*. Vashon Island, Wash.: Vashon Point Productions, 1986.

Sainsbury, John C. *Commercial Fishing Methods*. Farnham, Surrey, England: Fishing News Books Ltd., 1986.

Skalley, Michael. *Foss: Ninety Years of Towboating*. Burbank: Superior Publishing Co., 1986.

Upton, Joe. *Alaska Blues: A Fisherman's Journal*. Anchorage: Alaska Northwest Publishing Company, 1977.

Magazines
Pacific Fisherman
West Coast Mariner
WoodenBoat
WorkBoat

Did you enjoy this book?

Sasquatch Books publishes books and guides related to the Pacific Northwest. Our books are available at bookstores and other retail outlets throughout the region. Here is a partial list of our current titles.

Travel

Back Roads of Oregon
82 Trips on Oregon's Scenic Byways
Earl Thollander

Back Roads of Washington
74 Trips on Washington's Scenic Byways
Earl Thollander

Northern California Best Places
Restaurants, Lodgings, and Touring from Monterey Bay to Crescent City
Laura Hagar and Stephanie Irving

Northwest Best Places
Restaurants, Lodgings, and Touring in Oregon, Washington, and British Columbia
David Brewster and Stephanie Irving

Northwest Cheap Sleeps
Mountain Motels, Island Cabins, Ski Bunks, Beach Cottages, and Hundreds of Penny-pinching Travel Ideas for the Adventurous Road Tripper
Stephanie Irving

Portland Best Places
A Discriminating Guide to Portland's Restaurants, Lodgings, Shopping, Nightlife, Arts, Sights, Outings, and Annual Events
Kim Carlson and Stephanie Irving

Seattle Best Places
The Most Discriminating Guide to Seattle's Restaurants, Shops, Hotels, Nightlife, Sights, Outings, and Annual Events
David Brewster and Stephanie Irving

Seattle Cheap Eats
300 Terrific Bargain Eateries
Kathryn Robinson and Stephanie Irving

Seattle Survival Guide
The Essential Handbook for City Living (Absolutely Everything You Need to Know to Make Your Way Through the Urban Maze)
Theresa Morrow

Field Guides

Field Guide to the Bald Eagle
Includes Maps and Directions to Eagle-Watching Sites in Alaska, Baja California, British Columbia, California, Oregon, and Washington

Field Guide to the Gray Whale
With Maps and Directions to Land and Sea Whale-Watching Sites in Alaska, Baja California, British Columbia, California, Oregon, and Washington

Field Guide to the Grizzly Bear
Understanding and Safely Observing *Ursus arctos* in Western North America

Field Guide to the Orca
With Maps and Directions to Land and Sea Whale-Watching Sites Along the Pacific Coast from California to Alaska

Field Guide to the Pacific Salmon
Including Salmon-Watching Sites in Alaska, British Columbia, Washington, Oregon, and Northern California

Field Guide to the Sasquatch
Follow in the Footsteps of North America's Most Elusive Animal

For a complete catalog of Sasquatch books, or to inquire about ordering our books by phone or mail, please contact us at the address below.

Sasquatch Books
1931 Second Avenue
Seattle, WA 98101
(206)441-5555